SIMPLE HOME FURNISHINGS

SIMPLE HOME FURNISHINGS

50 fabulous ideas for transforming windows, chairs, sofas and beds

Isabel Stanley

Photography by James Duncan

southwater

This edition is published by Southwater

Distributed in the UK by
The Manning Partnership
251–253 London Road East
Batheaston
Bath BA1 7RL
tel. 01225 852 727
fax 01225 852 852

Published in the USA by
Anness Publishing Inc.
27 West 20th Street
Suite 504
New York
NY 10011
fax 212 807 6813

Distributed in Canada by
General Publishing
895 Don Mills Road
400–402 Park Centre
Toronto, Ontario M3C 1W3
tel. 416 445 3333
fax 416 445 5991

Distributed in Australia by
Sandstone Publishing
Unit 1, 360 Norton Street
Leichhardt
New South Wales 2040
tel. 02 9560 7888
fax 02 9560 7488

Southwater is an imprint of Anness Publishing Limited
Hermes House, 88–89 Blackfriars Road, London SE1 8HA
tel. 020 7401 2077; fax 020 7633 9499

© 1995, 2001 Anness Publishing Limited

Publisher: Joanna Lorenz
Editorial Manager: Helen Sudell
Designer: Lilian Lindblom
Jacket Design: The Bridgewater Book Company Limited
Photographer: James Duncan
Stylists: Theressa Allflatt, Kirsty Turner, and Lindy Leyton
Production Controller: Joanna King

Previously published as *Step-by-Step: 50 Cushions, Covers & Curtains*

1 3 5 7 9 10 8 6 4 2

CONTENTS

INTRODUCTION

If the notion of soft furnishings conjures up for you images of fussy flounces and frills in mass-produced fabrics, think again. Styles have changed and there is a new approach to interior design. Individual ideas can be catered for and schemes can be created around your personality, rather than being dictated by furnishing merchandizers. The possibilities are more exciting than you could ever imagine.

If you wish to redecorate an entire room, it's a good idea to spend time researching. Check out interior-design magazines for information and inspiration. Rather than trying to duplicate a look slavishly, use other's work to inspire a personal look. Note what types of fabric and furnishings produce an atmosphere or style.

A scheme can spring from your personal possessions. There might already be something wonderful in your home that will inspire you, such as a collection that you wish to display to its best advantage. Look at the style of furniture you have, the wall colour, the shape of the room and the amount of light. You may wish to change or disguise some aspects, to create the scheme you desire. However, it is better to work with the space you have, and enhance it, than to work against it. If you have a limited budget, use an inexpensive fabric, such as calico or muslin, for large expanses such as curtains or coverings, and use more expensive fabrics in smaller quantities, such as for cushion covers.

Begin your scheme plan by gathering swatches of fabrics, paying attention to their colour and texture. Make notes on which colours contrast and harmonize. Remember that your "canvas" is three-dimensional and that the furnishings will exist in a space. Try to regard the fabrics as different blocks of colour and to analyse their proportions in relation to each other.

Glossary of Fabrics

Brocade
Satin-weave fabric with a raised design, usually traditional, i.e. floral.
Fibres: Originally made from silk; now also produced in synthetics and cotton blends making them more durable and affordable.
Characteristics: Frays easily; drapes well.

Calico
Strong, coarse, plain-weave fabric, usually white or natural with brown flecks. Available in many weights and widths.
Fibres: Cotton.
Characteristics: Needs to be washed before making up, unless pre-shrunk. Washes and dyes well; however, press while damp, as it creases easily.

Cambric
A plain-weave and closely woven fabric, plain one side, with a sheen on the other.
Fibres: Cotton and linen.
Characteristics: Creases easily; press while damp.

Canvas or Duck
Plain-weave, coarse fabric, available in many colours and weights.
Fibres: Cotton.
Characteristics: Dyes well; difficult to sew because of hardness; inexpensive.

Chintz
Plain-weave, closely woven fabric. Plain on one side with a sheen; resin glaze on the other; sometimes printed with floral and bird motifs.
Fibres: Cotton.
Characteristics: Sheen repels dirt; to retain this quality the fabric must be dry-cleaned.

Corduroy
Plain-weave fabric with vertical pile-effect ribbing, varying in width from fine needlecord to broad or "jumbo".
Fibres: Cotton.
Characteristics: Strong, but pile will flatten and crease with use. Press while damp on a velvet pin board. Frays easily.

Crewel
Plain or multi-coloured chain-stitch floral or floral embroidery, on a plain background. Usually produced in India.
Fibres: Cotton with wool embroidery.
Characteristics: Heavy; needs dry-cleaning; embroidery susceptible to wear.

Damask
Usually a self-coloured fabric, with traditional woven satin-effect floral designs and plain-weave background. Can be overprinted.
Fibres: Originally silk, now produced in a variety of fibres and blends, mostly linen.
Characteristics: Expensive, depending on the fibre content.

Denim
Fabric usually dyed blue or black, but also available in white and pastels.
Fibres: Cotton.
Characteristics: Inexpensive, hard wearing, difficult to sew, fades with washing. Fabric softens with wear.

Gingham
Also a dressmaking fabric; alternating stripes of coloured and white threads in warp and weft, produce a checked pattern.
Fibres: Cotton or cotton blend.
Characteristics: Washes well.

Hessian (burlap)
A coarse, loosely woven fabric.
Fibres: Jute or jute/hemp blend.
Characteristics: Frays easily; inexpensive; should be pre-shrunk.

Holland
Plain-weave fabric stiffened with shellac.
Fibres: Cotton and linen.
Characteristics: Hard wearing.

Lace
Open-work fabric available in a variety of designs; may be bought in lengths or panels.
Fibres: Cotton; cotton/polyester blend; nylon and viscose (rayon).
Characteristics: Delicate, cannot withstand strain; not durable.

Lawn
Fine, crisp fabric.
Fibres: Cotton or cotton blend.
Characteristics: Smooth to the touch.

Linen
Loosely woven fabric made from uneven yarn.
Fibres: Linen is derived from natural flax; can be blended with cotton.
Characteristics: Expensive unless blended; hard wearing.

Moiré
A surface watermark finish, usually applied to fabric with a satin effect.
Fibres: Originally silk; now viscose (rayon) or cotton blend.
Characteristics: Because of finishing, may be delicate; will stain if in contact with water. Dry-clean; watermark will fade.

Muslin
White or natural open-weave, gauzy fabric.
Fibres: Cotton or cotton blend.
Characteristics: Dyes well; effective when gathered or layered.

Net
A mesh fabric.
Fibres: Cotton or synthetics.
Characteristics: Stiff; does not fray.

Organza
Gauzy, fine, stiff, slightly starchy; available in metallic finishes.
Fibres: Silk, polyester or viscose (rayon).
Characteristics: Crisp texture; looks good layered; press while damp.

Polyvinyl chloride or PVC (vinyl)
A plastic cloth, may be cotton-backed and patterned.
Fibres: Synthetic.
Characteristics: Water-resistant, wipeable. Spray a special lubricant on to sewing machine needle and foot before stitching.

Sailcloth
Plain or basket-weave, available plain, dyed and striped.
Fibres: Cotton, cotton/polyester blend.
Characteristics: Hard wearing; wash unless pre-shrunk. Press while damp.

Satin or sateen
Soft fabric with a surface sheen. Sateen sheen is more subtle than satin. Available in a variety of weights and colours.
Fibres: Cotton and cotton blends.
Characteristics: Hard wearing; dyes well.

Silk shantung
Woven with yarns of irregular thickness, to give an uneven surface.
Fibres: Originally silk, now made in cotton and synthetics.
Characteristics: Gathers and frills well.

Taffeta
Plain-weave fabric with a distinct sheen.
Fibres: Originally silk, now made from synthetics.
Characteristics: A crisp fabric; elaborate in appearance; frays easily.

Tartan
Woven, checked design; warp and weft have alternating stripes of coloured threads.
Fibres: Originally made in wool, now produced in silk and blends.
Characteristics: In wool and silk, tartan is hard wearing.

Ticking
Tightly woven herringbone fabric, with stripes; available in many weights and colours.
Fibres: Linen and cotton.
Characteristics: Hard wearing; difficult to sew; wash before making up, unless pre-shrunk.

Twill
Raised, diagonal ribbing produced by weaving.
Fibres: Cotton or wool; also blended with synthetics.
Characteristics: Hard wearing.

Velvet
Closely woven backing and dense-cut pile surface. Dress velvet is lighter and more lustrous.
Fibres: Originally made from silk; now produced in cotton and blended with synthetics.
Characteristics: Frays easily; difficult to handle. Cut out with care: the nap or lie of the pile must face in the same direction on all pieces.

Voile
Fine, lightweight fabric available plain and patterned.
Fibres: Cotton and silk can be blended with synthetics.
Characteristics: Drapes well.

Wool
Woven fleece; springy, warm texture.
Fibres: Blended with synthetics and cotton.
Characteristics: Prone to shrinkage, should not be used for articles which need regular washing. Expensive but less so when blended.

Soft-furnishing Materials

These soft materials can all be used to enhance
and complete your soft-furnishing projects.

Bias binding
Can be bought or hand-made.
Cut on the cross (diagonal),
these narrow strips can be used
to bind raw edges on curtains,
towels, blinds and table linen.

Bondaweb
A specialized, temporary, iron-
on, fusible film, used to hold
cut shapes on to the background fabric while stitching.

Boning
Used to suspend mosquito-net
bed drapes (pages 44–45).

Braid
Decorative woven ribbon, used
to trim cushions and upholstery.
Available in many designs,
colours, weights and widths.

Brass rings
Used to attach heading tapes to
curtain hooks, or tie-backs to
hooks.

Buckram
Stiffening fabric, used for pelmets (valances) and tie backs.

Buttons
Available in many sizes and
colours

Chain weights
Available in a variety of weights.
Used to weigh down net or
sheer curtains and heavy
curtains.

Curtain hooks
Hand-sewn to gathered
headings.

Curtain lining
Available in mostly pastel
colours; it has a slight sheen.

Curtain weights
Usually round or rectangular;
encased in fabric envelopes
inserted into curtain corners.

Curtain-heading tape
Available in a variety of widths;
stiffens curtain headings.

Embroidery thread
Available in many colours and
metallic finishes, in stranded
and perlé cotton.

Eyelets
Available in kit form, usually
used to head PVC (vinyl)
curtains. Can also be used to
head fabric curtains.

Fabric flowers and foliage
Delicate decorative embellish-
ments for tie-backs, table
settings and boxes.

Fringing
Cut fringing is used to trim
many soft furnishings.

Gathering tape
Curtain-heading tape that can
be pulled up to form gathers.

Interfacing
Used to stiffen fabric. Available
in black and white and fusible
iron-on and stitch-in varieties.

Interlining
Extra layer of fabric between
lining and main fabric. Available
in different thicknesses.

Lace
Open-weave edging, used to trim
sheer drapes, medium-weight
curtains and tablecloths.

Pencil-pleat tape
Curtain-heading tape that gives
close regular pleats.

Piping cord
Insert in seams to provide a
defining decorative feature on
upholstery, and loose cushion
covers.

Press-fasteners
Metallic fasteners for lightweight
fabrics and soft furnishings,
duvets and cushion covers.

Press-fastener tape
Quicker to apply than individual
fasteners.

Ribbon
Many colours, widths, patterns
and textures available; used for
trimming bed linen and table
linen.

Self-adhesive felt
A glue-backed felt, easily applied
to wood or card.

Thread
Match thread to fabric colour;
usually a slightly darker colour is
preferred. Also use silk for silk,
cotton for cotton.

Velcro
Hook and loop fastener that
presses together.

Wadding (batting)
Synthetic filling used to make
cushion pads.

Zip fasteners (zippers)
Comes in various weights and
colours with either plastic or the
stronger metallic teeth.

brass rings

self-adhesive felt

Buckram

wadding (batting)

zip fasteners (zippers)

bias binding

press-fasteners

velcro

press-fastener tape

fabric flowers

curtain hooks

fringing

curtain lining

thread

chain weights

curtain weights

embroidery thread

braid

boning

Bondaweb

eyelets

gathering tape

ribbon

piping cord

interlining

interfacing

curtain heading tape

Tools and Equipment

A small selection of equipment is required to make the soft furnishings in this book.

Corner turner
Useful tool for making crisp creases and turning points.

Craft knife
Lightweight sharp knife, with replaceable blades for cutting paper and card.

Fabric dyes
Cold-water dyes dye cotton, linen, viscose (rayon), wool and silk. Dying polyester and cotton blends produces a lighter shade; pure synthetics do not dye at all. Cold-water dyes need a fixing agent, such as vinegar or salt, to secure the colour. Fabrics with special finishes should not be dyed.
Hot-water dyes are suitable for all the above, plus nylon blends, although a lighter colour is produced. Wool is prone to shrinkage. Using a washing machine to dye fabric is recommended; it is clean and quick and produces an even colour. with few blemishes.

Fabric paints and pens
There is a wide range of easy-to-use products available; read manufacturer's instructions and buy those that are water-based and fixed by ironing. Choose from plain colours, metallic, opaque, glittery, puffy, shiny or fluorescents. Paints can be mixed and are applied with brushes, pens are easier and cleaner to use.

Gauge
Ruler with a marker that can be set to indicate a measurement.

Iron
Use the heaviest iron that is able to reach a high temperature. It should have steam and spray controls.

Markers
Soft lead pencil can be used to trace a design or use a vanishing fabric-marking pen. Some fade in contact with water; however, those that fade on exposure to air are recommended.

Needles
These are available in many sizes. Use specialized needles with wide eyes when working with strands of wool or embroidery thread.

Pinking shears
For finishing seams on upholstery, to prevent fraying.

Pins and pin cushion
Fine and medium-weight pins are the most useful; heavy pins are used for loose covers and heavy fabrics. Use a pin cushion to keep pins to hand.

Ruler
A yardstick or metre rule made from wood or metal is useful to measure fabric lengths accurately.

Scissors
For snipping and embroidery purposes, use scissors with 9–10 cm (3–4 in) blades. Use heavy scissors with 20–22 cm (8–9 in) blades for cutting out.

Set square (carpenter's square)
Use for squaring fabrics, usually hems and seams. ·

Sewing machine
Basic sewing machine with normal stitching foot, zip foot, piping foot and darning foot.

Skewer
Used while cutting heavy fabrics to hold fabric in place on the work top.

Staple gun
Use special heavyweight stapler to apply fabric to wood, when covering pelmets and screens.

Stencil paper or card
Available from artists' suppliers, stencil paper is pliable and has a waxy surface. Card (cardboard) can be used instead.

Stitch-ripper
Quickly unpicks stitches.

Tape measure
Flexible ruler made from cloth or plastic, used to measure fabric and around curves

Thimble
Used to protect fingers while sewing heavy fabrics.

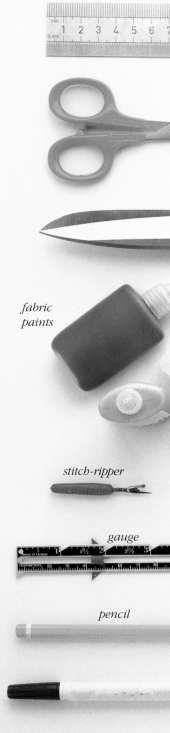

fabric paints

stitch-ripper

gauge

pencil

fabric marker

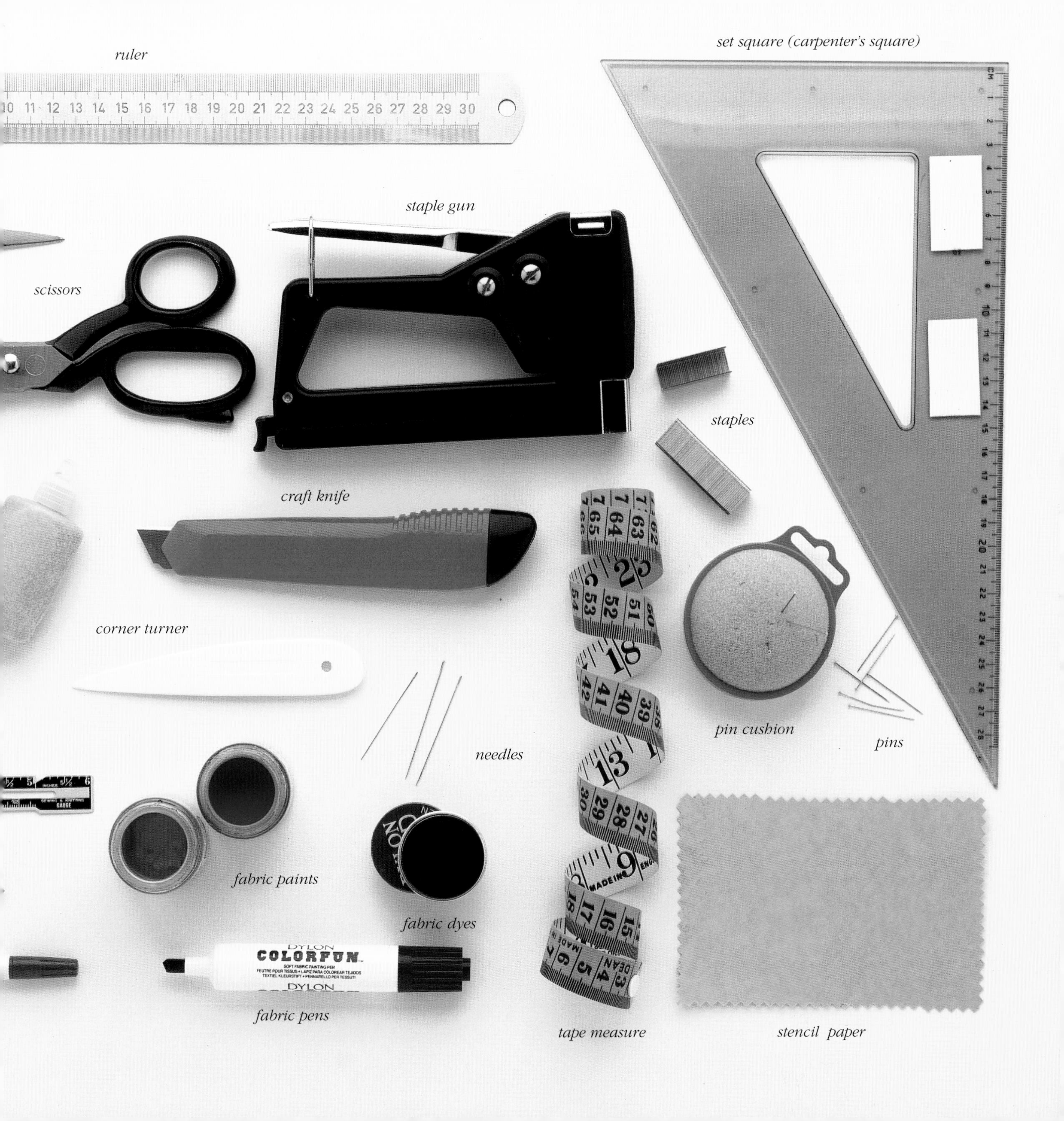

ruler

set square (carpenter's square)

staple gun

scissors

staples

craft knife

corner turner

pin cushion

pins

needles

fabric paints

DYLON
COLORFUN™
SOFT FABRIC PAINTING PEN
FEUTRE POUR TISSUS • LAPIZ PARA COLOREAR TEJIDOS
TEXTIEL KLEURSTIFT • PENNARELLO PER TESSUTI
DYLON

fabric dyes

fabric pens

tape measure

stencil paper

Selecting Fabrics

There is no need to head straight for furnishing-fabric sections. Many dress fabrics are suitable for soft furnishings: calico, canvas and sailcloth can be bought inexpensively from artists' equipment outlets or sailing-boat suppliers. Unusual fabrics can be found in markets, sales, secondhand or charity shops and car-boot or tag sales.

Practical as well as aesthetic considerations must inform your choice. Characteristics such as the weave, fibre content and weight will affect a fabric's ability to withstand wear and tear and dictate its suitability to a particular type of furnishing. When choosing a fabric, consider the following points:

1 Check the effect of a large amount of fabric, especially if it is heavily patterned. It may be advisable to buy a metre to take home to view in place.

2 Examine the fabric in both natural and artificial light.

3 Consider the weight; this will dictate not only how the fabric drapes but also how much light it will allow through and how much wear it will bear.

4 Read the manufacturer's tag for information on stain-resistance and laundering instructions. Fabrics that are not pre-shrunk need to be laundered before use.

5 Consider the texture: smooth/cool fabrics are required for sheeting; warm/soft fabrics are more suitable for loose covers or throws.

6 Check for creasing. Crumple up a small amount in your hand to see how quickly the creases fall out. Fabrics that retain creases are unsuitable for covers.

7 Pull some threads away from the raw edge to see how it frays; this will affect how you finish seams and hems.

8 Once your decision is made and the fabric is being measured, examine it for flaws. Ask for extra fabric if you find any. Ensure you buy sufficient fabric to start with, because new batches might exhibit variations of colour.

Fabric Quantities

You will often find the width of the chosen fabric is insufficient, so a number of widths have to be joined together. Divide the cut width by the width of the fabric, to calculate the number of widths required. Multiply this figure by the cut length to find the amount of fabric required.

If the item is lined, buy lining as wide as the outer fabric. When joining the widths for bed linen or tablecloths, avoid a central seam; if two widths are required, split the second width in half lengthways and join each half on either side of the first.

Allowance for Patterned Fabric

If curtains are made from patterned fabric, particularly a large design, allow enough extra fabric so that patterns match when widths are made up. To calculate how much extra fabric is needed, divide the cut length of the curtain by the length of the pattern repeat and round this number up to next full figure.

Joining Patterned Fabrics

1 Lay the lengths of fabric on the floor or table, right-side up. Press under the selvedge and 1 cm (½ in) to the wrong side on one width. Line the second piece up to the fold on the first, accurately matching the patterns; pin them together with the fold just covering the selvedge. On the edge of the folded piece, carefully ladder stitch two widths together.

2 Fold the first side over and machine stitch the seam.

Measuring for Curtains

Measurements should be taken with a steel ruler or tape measure. Fittings such as the track or pole and carpet should be in place during measuring; they will have a bearing on the overall drop of the curtain, that is, the finished length. To find the cut length (the amount of fabric required to make one curtain drop), headings, hems and the "hook" drop need to be estimated.

A selection of curtain tracks and poles

Length or "hook" drop

The pole or track is usually fixed 15 cm (6 in) above the window, extending 15 cm (6 in) at either end. Measurements should be taken from the bottom of the pole to the floor; that is the "hook" drop. Curtains can just brush the floor, in which case deduct 1.5 cm (⅝ in) from the hook drop. Or they can drape on the floor: add 5–7 cm (2–3 in) to the hook drop. For a sill-length curtain, measure to the top of the sill and add 5 cm (2 in). If the sill protrudes, subtract 1.5 cm (⅝ in).

Hems

Details are given for each project. Generally, for a lined full-length curtain, add 20 cm (8 in) [a 10 cm (4 in) wide double hem]. For net or lightweight curtains, add 10 cm (4 in) [a 5 cm (2 in) wide double hem].

Widths

The length of the pole or track will dictate the width of the curtain.

Fullness

The required fullness will depend on the heading and fabric used. The length of the pole or track should be multiplied by the fullness allowance, to find the overall width.

Width Hems

In general, side hems are 2 cm (¾ in) wide double hems; 8 cm (4 in) should be added to the overall width, to find the cut width.

Right: A selection of cushions and throws featured in this book.

TECHNIQUES

Preparing Fabric

It is important to cut fabrics accurately and hold them firmly in position with tacking (basting) stitches or pins before stitching. Save time and avoid mistakes and wasted fabric – and achieve a more professional appearance – by following these recommendations.

Cutting out

Before cutting, check for flaws such as dye spots, pulled . threads or mistakes in printing or weaving. Either return the fabric to the shop or work around it. Some fabrics have not been pre-shrunk; these will need to be washed before cutting, in case of shrinkage. Lay the fabric on the table or floor and use shears to cut out the pieces.

1 To cut lengthways, fold the fabric and match the selvedges. Otherwise, use a set square (carpenter's square) to cut the cloth on the square. To do this, place the square at right angles to the selvedges and mark the cutting line.

2 To cut loosely woven fabrics on the square, pull away a weft (crossways) thread to use as a guideline before cutting.

Pinning

Insert pins so that they can be easily removed when stitching, i.e. pinheads should point towards front of machine. Pins can also be placed at right angles to the seam to stop the fabric shifting.

Pressing

Press into the seams from each side with steam; do not press over seams.

Scaling-up Templates (patterns)

The templates (patterns) featured in this book may not be to the size you require, in which case they must be redrawn. To make a design or shape larger than the template, scale it up using graph paper. Use a scale such as one square on the template to two squares on the graph paper, or whatever suits your need.

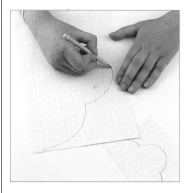

1 Using an appropriate scale, enlarge the template (pattern) on to a sheet of graph paper by copying the shape from each small square on to the larger sheet.

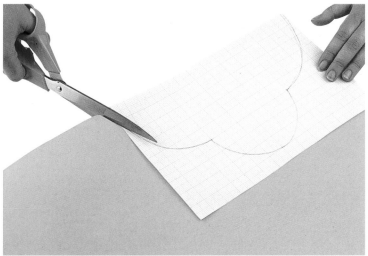

2 Cut out the new template (pattern) and transfer it to card.

Hand Stitches

Tacking stitch (basting stitch)

A temporary stitch, used to hold fabric in position while machine stitching.

Herringbone stitch

A hemming stitch used on heavier fabrics and single hems. The stitch is invisible on the right side. Work it from left to right. Anchor on, and on the hem and through the single layer, sew one stitch backwards, picking up just a few threads. Then move the needle diagonally across the folded hem, make another back stitch, cross the needle over the preceding stitch and pick up a few threads on the single layer.

Slip stitch

Most commonly used to hold hems on lighter fabrics in place. Work it from left to right. It should be invisible, so only pick up a few threads when stitching. Do not pull the stitch too tight, or the hem will pucker.

Ladder stitch

A stitch used to join folded edges together. To ensure they butt (meet) up together neatly, make a stitch horizontally from and to each folded edge; make stitches through the fold.

Gathering stitch

A temporary stitch, to prepare fabric for permanent stitching. Double up the thread and sew a running stitch 1 cm (½ in) from the raw edge.

Stab stitch

A simple stitch, invisible on the right side, that is used to hold a cord or several layers of loosely arranged fabric in place. Bring the needle up through the material from the underside and down again, almost in the same place, to catch a tiny amount of material.

Lock stitch

To join curtain-fabric lining and interlining together loosely. With wrong sides together, pin the centre line. Fold the lining back over the pin line. Working from left to right, make a stitch through the folded edge and the curtain fabric. It should be invisible, so only pick up a few threads. Take the needle over the preceding stitch and then insert it 5 cm (2 in) to the right.

Seams

The choice of seam depends mainly on the type of fabric and the position of the seam.

Straight Seam
The most common seam.

With right sides pinned or tacked (basted) together, machine stitch 2 cm (¾ in) (unless otherwise stated) from the raw edges. Remove pins or tacking. Finish raw edges with pinking shears or work a zigzag machine stitch.

CRAFT TIP
The raw edges of the seam allowance should neatened to prevent fraying. Edges may be finished with an open zigzag stitch. The quickest way is to use pinking shears but this is not hardwearing. The most secure and attractive method is to apply bias binding. Press the seam open.

French Seam
A neat way of joining fine or easily frayed unlined fabrics because the raw edges are enclosed within the seam. Not suitable for heavy fabrics.

1 With wrong sides together, stitch a seam 9 mm (⅜ in) from the raw edges. Trim to 4 mm (³⁄₁₆ in) from the seam line.

2 Turn the work right sides out, with the seam inside. Stitch on the actual required seam line. The fold should be 6 mm (³⁄₁₆ in) wide.

Lapped Seam
A method of joining interlining and interfacing neatly that also minimizes bulk.

Overlap one raw edge over the other and machine stitch a zigzag through the two layers. Trim back the raw edges to the stitching.

Corners and Curves

To allow a seam or hem to lie flat, it is sometimes necessary to snip into seam allowances, usually cutting a triangular shape away. Take care not to snip the stitching.

Hems

To save time when making a hem, simply ensure the fabric is cut straight, so the hem can be folded and pressed without pinning or tacking. Hems can be held in place invisibly with slip stitch or herringbone stitch, or visibly with machine stitching.

Single Hems
On a curtain that is to be lined, a simple single hem can be sewn.

Fold and press in a turning of 5 cm (2 in). Mitre the corners and secure the hem with herringbone stitch.

Double Hems
Most curtains have a double hem of 10 cm (4 in), in case they need to be lengthened.

1 Press up the hem allowance on the wrong side of the curtain. Open the hem out.

2 Fold raw edge to pressing line. Press. Press hem up and slip stitch or herringbone stitch folded edge to main curtain.

Weighting Curtains
Special weights concealed inside hems enable curtains to drape well. A chain weight should be sewn into the lower fold of a sheer curtain with small stitches. Single round or rectangular lead weights should be sewn into "pockets" made from scrap fabric and slip stitched into the hem.

Mitred Corners

This technique is used when two hems join at a corner. To form neat, flat corners, mitring (joining) should be carried out before permanent stitching.

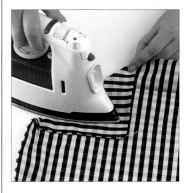

1 Turn and press in hems; open out folds. Turn and press the corner so that the diagonal fold passes through where the finished corner will be.

2 Re-fold the hem to form a diagonal seam. Insert a weight at this point if required.

3 Join the folded edges with ladder stitch. Stitch the hem.

Bias Binding

Hems and seams can be easily neatened with bias binding, which encloses the raw edges and can be a decorative feature. Bias binding can be purchased or home-made.

1 Cut a rectangular piece of fabric. Find the bias by folding the fabric diagonally. Mark this fold with pins.

2 Using these pins as a guide, mark fabric with parallel lines 4 cm (1½ in) apart, marking as many strips as needed. Trim off the two triangular corners.

3 Join the shorter ends right sides together. Pin them together, so that the end of one strip extends beyond the join at the top and bottom. Stitch a 6 mm (⅜ in) seam and press it open. Cut along the marked lines.

1 Make a strip of bias binding. Fold and pin the fabric over the cord. Tack (baste) and machine stitch with a piping-cord foot.

To Apply Bias Binding

1 With fabric and binding right sides together, pin the binding 1.5 cm (⅝ in) from the edge all round. Stitch the seam line 1 cm (½ in) from the raw edges.

2 Trim to 4 mm (⅜ in) from the stitching line. Press the binding out on the right sides, turn and accurately press the binding edges under 1 cm (½ in).

3 Fold the binding over and slip stitch it in position.

2 Starting at an unobtrusive place, pin the cord all round, with the cord facing inwards and matching the raw edges of the bias binding and the fabric. To join the piping cord, trim away the encased cord and lap one end of the casing over the other. Slip stitch it to secure.

Closures and Fastenings

The right choice of closure or fastening depends on a variety of factors: type of fabric, position of the seam and wear of the furnishing.

Inserting a Zip (zipper)

Zips (zippers) are suitable for cushions and are good for curved seams. The type of fabric dictates the weight of zip to use.

1 Mark the position of zip (zipper) on the seam. Machine stitch or tack (baste) the seam in which the zip is to be fitted. Use a large machine stitch length; these are temporary stitches. Press the seam allowance open.

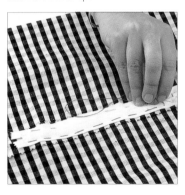

2 Tack the zip (zipper) to the wrong side of the seam, ensuring that the zip is centred over the seam.

3 Using the machine's zipper foot, top stitch all around the zip, along each side and across either end. With a stitch-ripper, carefully unpick (take out) the temporary stitches.

Attaching Press Fastenings

These metal fastenings that press together are suitable for bed linen and cushions.

Turn and press a double hem. Machine stitch it. Stitch two halves of fastenings one on each side of closure, ensuring that pairs match up. Top stitch an X at each end of closure through both hems.

Attaching Velcro and Press-fastener (iron-on fastener) Tape

Suitable for fastenings on bed linen.

1 Turn and press a double hem the width of the Velcro or tape on each piece of fabric where the opening should be. Place the two halves of the Velcro one on each hem and machine-stitch the hem and Velcro, or tape, in place on each half.

2 To secure the opening, top stitch an X figure at each end of the closure, through both hems after making up.

Buttonhole Closure

Suitable for both bed linen and cushions.

1 Turn and press a double hem at least 1 cm (½ in) wider than the button. Machine-stitch it. The buttonhole length is the diameter of the button plus 4 mm (³/₁₆ in). Mark the positions of the buttons on the underlap (underneath) and the buttonholes on the overlap with fabric marker. Match up marks.

2 Work a close zigzag machine stitch along one marked edge of each button hole. Set the dial to a wider stitch and work a bar of six stitches. Reset the dial and stitch back along the marked edge. Work a bar at this end and back-stitch to secure. Insert the sharp end of a stitch-ripper into one end of the mark, between the stitched edges, and carefully make a slit.

TEMPLATES (PATTERNS)

These templates (patterns) are used in some of the projects in the book. You can either trace them directly from the page or make them as large or small as you like.

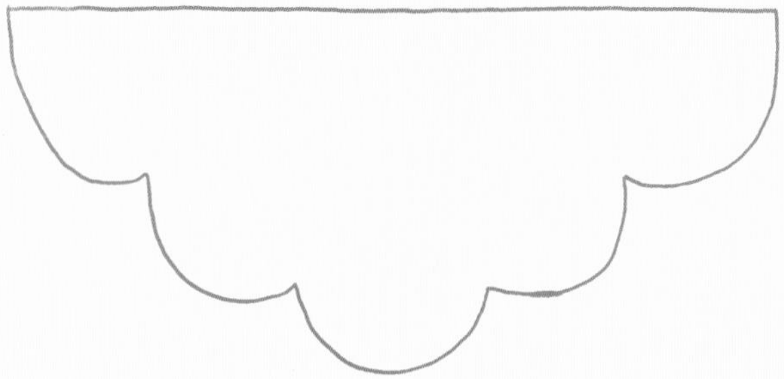

Painted Tablecloth with Scalloped Edging

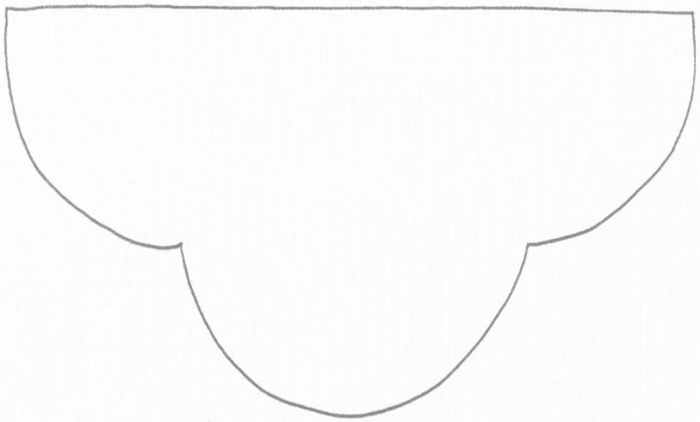

Shelf Edging

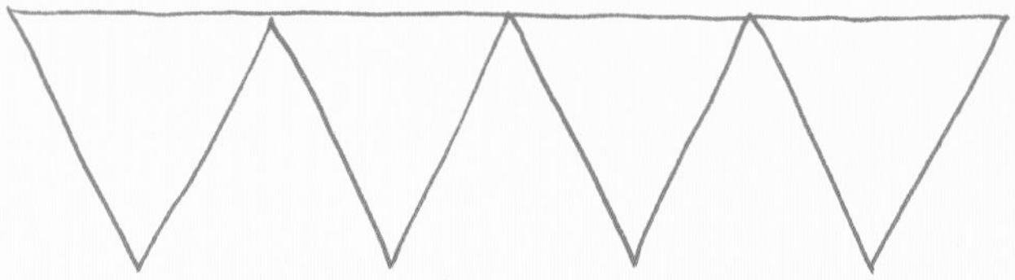

Picot Edged Pillowcase

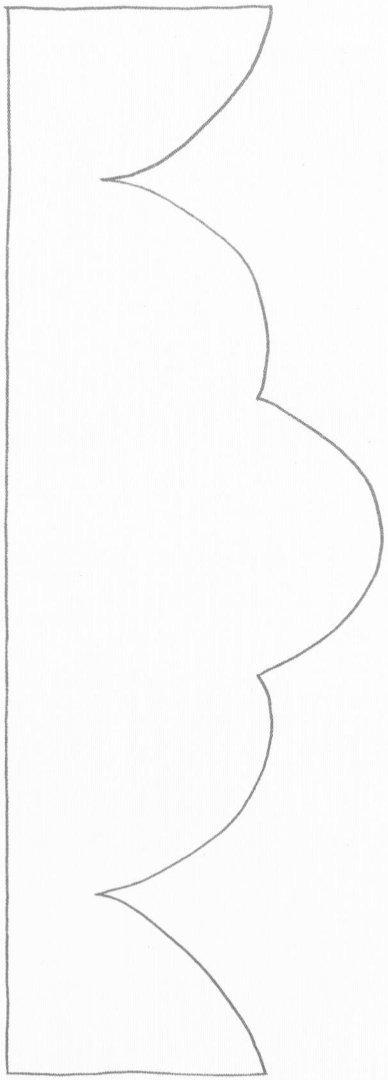

Valance

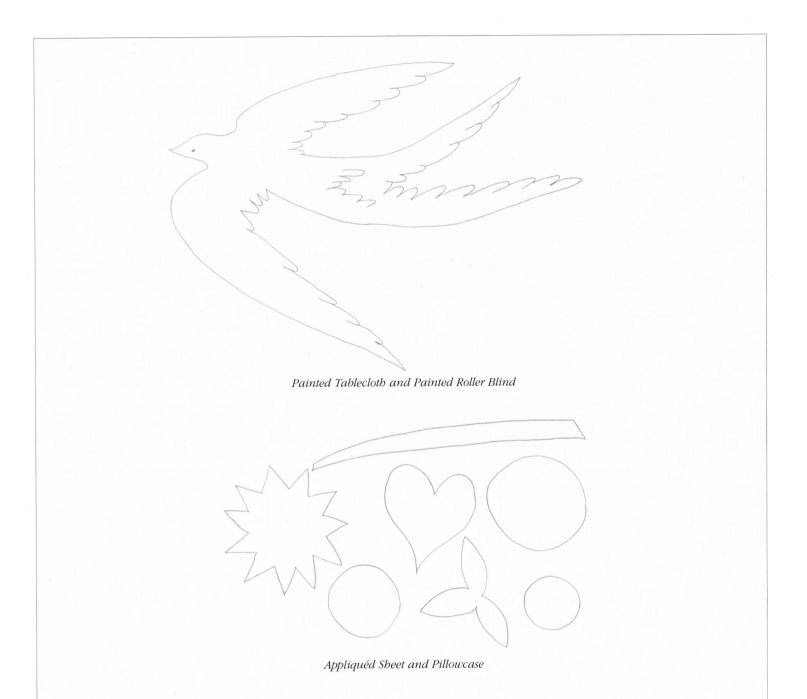

Painted Tablecloth and Painted Roller Blind

Appliquéd Sheet and Pillowcase

Self-bordered Organza and Satin Cushion Cover

Two layers of fabric are used to create this cushion cover. The pad is covered with brightly coloured satin, and the impact is diffused by a second cover of translucent fabric.

YOU WILL NEED

MATERIALS
square cushion pad
satin
matching thread
press-fasteners
organza
gold thread

EQUIPMENT
tape measure
scissors
iron
sewing machine
pins
fabric marker
needles

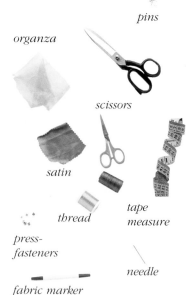

organza

pins

scissors

satin

thread

tape measure

press-fasteners

needle

fabric marker

1 For the top, cut one piece of satin to the size of the pad plus 2 cm (¾ in) all round. For the underside, cut two pieces of satin, each to half the size of the pad, plus a 2 cm (¾ in) seam allowance all round and an extra 2 cm (¾ in) overlap on one edge of both pieces. Turn and press a 1 cm (½ in) double hem on the centre edges. Machine stitch it. Put the top and underside pieces right sides together, overlapping the underside pieces. Pin and machine stitch all round.

2 Clip the corners and turn right sides out. On the opening edges, mark and stitch pairs of press-fasteners at intervals, ensuring each pair matches up.

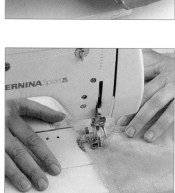

3 For the top of the outer cover, cut a piece of organza fabric to the size of the pad plus 10 cm (4 in) (the width of the border) and a 2 cm (¾ in) seam allowance all round. For the underside, cut two pieces of fabric each to half the size of the top plus a 2 cm (¾ in) overlap allowance on one side edge of both pieces. Turn and press a double hem of 1 cm (½ in) width on the centre edges of the underside. Assemble the top and undersides right sides together, overlapping the underside pieces. Pin and machine stitch, using gold thread, all round the seam.

4 Trim away the seam allowance to 5 mm (¼ in) from the stitching and clip the corners. Turn the work right sides out, press and top stitch all around, 6 mm (⁵⁄₁₆ in) from the edge.

5 On the top, mark a line 8.5 cm (3½ in) from the edge all round. Machine stitch along the marked line.

6 On the opening edges, mark and stitch pairs of press-fasteners at intervals, ensuring each pair matches up. Put the cushion pad into the satin cover and fasten it and then stuff the satin-covered cushion into the organza cover and fasten the outer cover.

Flag Cushion

This flag cushion is made up in a similar way to a patchwork cushion. Make a card template (pattern) before cutting out the triangular pieces.

YOU WILL NEED

MATERIALS
underside fabric
rectangular cushion pad
zip (zipper)
thread
card
1 piece each of pink, red, light blue and white fabric
tacking (basting) thread
embroidery thread (about 8 skeins)

EQUIPMENT
scissors
tape measure
card
pencil
ruler
craft knife or scalpel
pins
sewing machine
iron

fabrics

tape measure

pins

embroidery thread

card

scissors

needle

zip (zipper)

thread

craft knife

1 For the underside cut two pieces of fabric, each half the size of the pad plus 2 cm (¾ in) all round. Insert the zip (zipper) into the longest seam, to make a zipped opening. Cut card to the size of the cushion pad; mark diagonal lines from corner to corner. Cut out the shapes in different-colour fabrics, adding 2 cm (¾ in) allowance all round.

2 With right sides together, pin, tack (baste) and machine stitch two pieces along the edges that will form the diagonal seams. Press the seams open.

3 With right sides together, pin, tack (baste) and machine stitch the joined pieces along the other diagonal edges. Press the seams open.

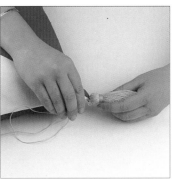

4 With underside and top right sides together, pin and machine stitch all around. Clip the corners. Reverse and insert the pad. Make tassels (see pages 58-9) for each corner.

Waterproof Cushion Covers

These cushion covers are easy to clean and ideal for taking on picnics or for using in the garden.

YOU WILL NEED

MATERIALS
cushion pad
PVC (vinyl) or fabric-backed
 PVC
matching thread
popper (snap fastener) kit

EQUIPMENT
tape measure
scissors
pins
sewing machine
hammer

scissors

PVC

tape
measure

poppers

hammer

thread

pins

1 Measure the cushion pad. For the top, cut one piece of PVC (vinyl) to this size, plus 2 cm (¾ in) all round as a seam allowance. Cut two pieces each to half this size, plus 2 cm (¾ in) all round as a seam and hem allowance. To make the fringing, measure around the seam-line of the top and cut one piece of 12 cm (4¾ in) wide fabric to this length, plus 4 cm (1½ in). Fold it in half lengthways and make 4 cm (1½ in) cuts into the folded edge, 1 cm (½ in) apart along the length.

2 With right sides facing, pin the fringing all around the top piece. Machine stitch all around the seam.

3 On the underside pieces, turn a double hem of 1 cm (½ in) width on the centre edges. Machine stitch the hem. On the opening edges, mark the position of pairs of poppers (snap fasteners), ensuring each pair matches up. Use the assembling tool and a hammer to attach the poppers to the opening edges. Assemble the top and undersides right sides together, overlapping the underside pieces. Pin and machine stitch all around the seam. Clip the corners and turn them right sides out and insert the cushion pad.

Woollen Cushion Cover

A cosy cushion that can be made without a sewing machine. Buttons and buttonhole closures can be an attractive feature on any cushion cover or pillowcase.

YOU WILL NEED

MATERIALS
cushion pad
woollen fabric
thread
embroidery thread
buttons

EQUIPMENT
tape measure
scissors
iron
pins
needle
sewing machine (optional)
fabric marker or pencil

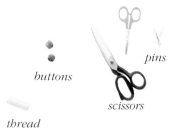

buttons

pins

scissors

thread

needle

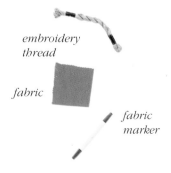

embroidery thread

fabric

fabric marker

1 Measure the cushion pad. For the top of the cushion, cut a piece of fabric to the size of the pad plus 10 cm (4 in) (the width of the border), and a 2 cm (¾ in) seam allowance all round. For the underside, cut two pieces, each to half the same size as the top, plus a 7.5 cm (3 in) opening and overlap allowance on one side edge of both pieces. On the underside pieces, turn and press under a 3 cm (1⅛ in) double hem on the centre edges. Pin and work a hand-sewn running stitch to hold the hem in place.

2 Assemble the top and underside pieces right sides together, overlapping the underside pieces. Pin and machine stitch or hand stitch around the seam. Press the seams. Clip the corners and turn the work right sides out.

3 Insert pins around the folded edge. Mark a line 10 cm (4 in) from the edge all round. Work a running stitch in embroidery thread along the line. Work two more parallel lines 1 cm (½ in) apart around the marked line.

4 Work a neat blanket stitch on the fold line: mark out the needle-entry points with a fabric marker or sharp pencil. Make the marks 2 cm (¾ in) from the folded edge and 1 cm (½ in) apart. Insert the needle in the first point, catch the thread behind the needle, pull the needle through and repeat.

5 On the underlap (underneath), mark the three button positions. Stitch in place. On the overlap, mark the buttonhole positions; make them 3–4 mm (⅛–³⁄₁₆ in) longer than the buttons, so that the marks match up. Snip a slit and work a blanket stitch around the raw edges. Insert the cushion pad.

Bolster Cushion

This sumptuous cushion can be trimmed with ribbon and lined or left unlined. Tie at either end with cord or ribbon.

YOU WILL NEED

MATERIALS
bolster cushion pad
fabric
tacking (basting) thread
wide ribbon for border
thread
lining fabric (optional)
cord or ribbon

EQUIPMENT
tape measure
scissors
pins
needle
sewing machine

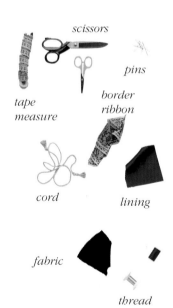

scissors

pins

tape measure

border ribbon

cord

lining

fabric

thread

1 Measure the length and circumference of the cushion pad. Cut one piece of fabric to the length plus 60 cm (24 in) and the circumference plus 4 cm (1¾ in). Lay the fabric face-up on a table and mark the position of the cushion pad. Pin and tack (baste) the ribbon 15 cm (6 in) in from either end.

2 Machine stitch the ribbon in place, using an open zigzag stitch.

3 Fold the outer fabric in half lengthways, right sides together, and machine stitch the long seam. To line the cover, cut a piece of lining fabric to the same size as the outer fabric. Fold in half lengthways and machine stitch the long seam.

4 With the right sides together, slip the lining tube over the fabric tube and pin and machine stitch one side edge. Open out the seam and pin the other side edges of the lining and the fabric right-sides together. Machine stitch the seam, leaving a gap of 15 cm (6 in).

5 Turn right sides out through the gap. Turn and press the opening edges under. Slip stitch the gap closed.

6 Insert the cushion pad, and centre it. Gather each end and wrap a length of cord around. The cord ends can be knotted or finished with a tassel (see pages 58–9).

Knitted Cushion

Basket-weave stitch creates an interesting texture for this unusual cushion cover. The pattern is designed to fit a cushion 30 x 30 cm (12 x 12 in).

YOU WILL NEED

MATERIALS
200 g lambswool yarn
30 x 30 cm (12 x 12 in)
 cushion pad

EQUIPMENT
4.5 mm (US 6) knitting needles
cable needle
darning needle
scissors

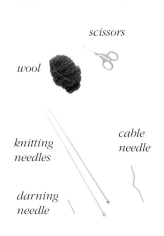

scissors

wool

knitting needles

cable needle

darning needle

1 Using two strands of yarn twisted together, cast on 72 stitches.
1st row Knit
2nd row Purl

2 3rd row Knit 3. Slip 3 stitches on to a cable needle and hold at the back of the work. Knit 3.

3 Knit 3 from the cable needle. Repeat to the end of the row; knit the remaining 3 stitches.

4 4th row Purl
5th row Knit
6th row Purl
7th row Knit 3. Slip 3 stitches on to the cable needle, hold at the front of the work, knit 3 and then knit 3 from the cable needle. Repeat to the end of the row; knit the remaining 3 stitches.
8th row Purl
Repeat until you have done 84 rows.
Cast off.

5 For the underside cast on 66.
1st row Knit
2nd row Purl
Repeat until you have done 84 rows and then cast off.
With wrong sides together, chain stitch through both layers. To work a chain stitch, insert the needle through both layers, loop the yarn under the point of the needle and make the stitch. Work the chain stitch around three sides.

6 Insert the cushion pad and work a chain stitch along the fourth side. Make four tassels with the yarn (see pages 58–9) and stitch one to each corner.

Seat Cushion Trimmed with Piping Cord

Make a wooden chair more comfortable with a tie-on seat cushion. Bows hold it in place.

YOU WILL NEED

MATERIALS
paper
wadding (batting)
white thread
calico (cotton fabric for pad)
outer fabric
piping cord
matching thread
zip (zipper)

EQUIPMENT
scissors
sewing machine
tape measure
needle
pins
iron

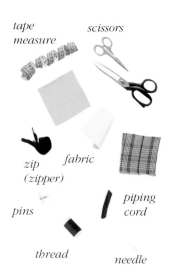

tape measure

scissors

zip (zipper)

fabric

pins

piping cord

thread

needle

1 Place a piece of paper on the seat and fold it back on itself along the edges of the seat. Ensure this template is symmetrical. Cut six pieces of wadding to the size of the template. Sew through the layers of wadding with a zigzag machine stitch.

2 Use the template (pattern) to cut two pieces of calico cotton; add a 2 cm (¾ in) seam allowance. Right sides together, stitch a seam all around, leaving a gap of 20 cm (8 in) at the back. Turn right sides out and insert the wadding.

3 Use the template (pattern) to cut two pieces of outer fabric; add a 2 cm (¾ in) seam allowance. Right sides facing, pin and tack (baste) piping cord around the top piece. Tuck the ends of the piping cord into the seam allowance. Stitch with zipper foot.

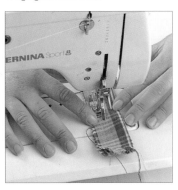

4 Clip corners and curves. For the ties, cut four pieces of fabric 60 × 10 cm (24 × 4 in). Fold them in half lengthways, right-sides together, and stitch along the long edge and one short edge. Clip the corners, turn right-sides out and press.

5 Position and pin the raw edges of the ties on either side of the chair legs. Assemble the top and underside pieces, right sides together. Using the zipper foot, machine stitch the seam all round, leaving a gap of 20 cm (8 in) at the back. Clip the corners and curves.

6 Turn the work right sides out. Sew the zipper to the opening edges by hand or machine. Insert the cushion pad.

Woven-ribbon Cushion

Brightly coloured satin ribbons will add a
wonderful splash of colour to any sofa or chair.

YOU WILL NEED

MATERIALS
cushion pad
satin fabric
zip (zipper)
matching thread
Bondaweb
satin ribbons

EQUIPMENT
tape measure
scissors
sewing machine
iron
pins

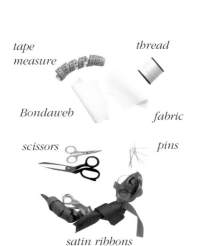

tape measure   *thread*

Bondaweb   *fabric*

scissors   *pins*

satin ribbons

zip (zipper)

1 For the top, cut one piece of satin to
the size of the pad, plus 2 cm (¾ in) all
round. For the underside, cut two pieces
of fabric half the size of the pad, plus
2 cm (¾ in) all round. Sew the zip in the
central seam. Press a piece of Bondaweb,
same size as pad, face-down on the right
side of the top fabric. Peel away backing.

2 Cut the ribbons to the length of
the top fabric. Pin the ribbons to two
sides of the fabric, 1 cm (½ in) from the
edges. Weave the ribbons under and
over, pulling them taut. Pin them in
place at the other ends.

3 Machine stitch all round the seam
to secure the ribbon ends. Using a hot
iron, press the top piece, fusing the
woven ribbons in place.

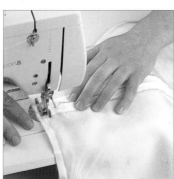

4 Undo the zip (zipper) in the piece
underneath. Assemble the top and
underside (bottom) fabrics, right sides
together. Pin and machine stitch all
round the seam. Clip the corners. Turn
the cover right sides out and insert the
cushion pad.

Woollen Chair Cover

This simple cover can be made without a sewing machine. Choose a soft wool fabric.

YOU WILL NEED

MATERIALS
fabric
embroidery thread
thread
ribbon

EQUIPMENT
tape measure
scissors
pins
darning needle
pencil or fabric marker
needle

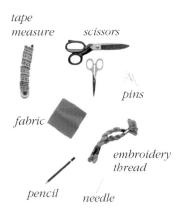

tape measure   *scissors*

pins

fabric

embroidery thread

pencil   *needle*

1 Measure widths of back and front of the chair and seat; use lesser width for cover. Measure depth of overhangs back and front, including seat, for final length. Cut two pieces of fabric to size and assemble. Mark knot positions about 12 cm (4¾ in) apart with pins.

2 Thread six lengths of embroidery thread onto darning needle. Insert it at a pin and pull through both layers of fabric, leaving an end 5 cm (2 in) long. Make a stitch on the wrong side, bring needle through to the right side. Tie a small knot with the two sections and trim the strands down to 3 cm (1¼ in) in length.

3 To work a neat blanket stitch, mark out the position of the needle entry points with a sharp pencil or fabric marker; make the marks 2 cm (¾ in) from the raw edges and 1 cm (½ in) apart. Anchor on, insert the needle in the first point, catch the thread behind the needle, pull the needle through and repeat the stitch. Repeat all round.

4 Cut six lengths of ribbon 40 cm (16 in), cutting the ends at an angle. Fold it in half widthways and insert the folded ends between the layers of fabric, at the corners. Pin and slip stitch in place. Arrange the cover on the chair and position remaining ties front and back. Slip stitch in place. Fasten the ties in bows.

Dining-room Chair Cover

An ordinary chair can be transformed with an imaginative cover. A kitchen chair is here disguised with a seat cushion and a skirt with inverted pleats at the corner points, and a padded back rest.

YOU WILL NEED

MATERIALS
paper
wadding (batting)
white thread
calico (cotton fabric for pad)
fabric
matching thread
ribbon
zip (zipper)
cardboard

EQUIPMENT
scissors
sewing machine
tape measure
needles
pencil
iron
pins

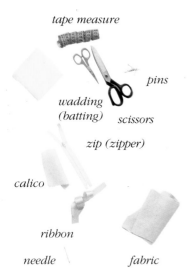

tape measure

pins

wadding (batting)   *scissors*

zip (zipper)

calico

ribbon

needle   *fabric*

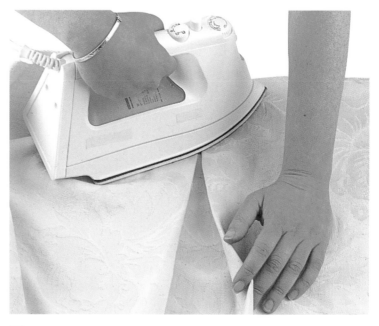

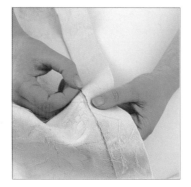

1 To make a cushion pad, follow steps 1 and 2 of the Seat Cushion Trimmed with Piping Cord (pages 32–3). Mark on the template (pattern) the points of the chair back struts and the front corners. For the skirt length, measure the depth of fall from the top of the seat to the floor. For the side panel of the skirt, measure the distance from the back of the chair leg to the front corner point. Cut two pieces of fabric to this length, plus a 2 cm (¾ in) seam allowance and a 10 cm (4 in) hem allowance, by the width measurement, plus a 4 cm (1½ in) side hem allowance and a 24 cm (9½ in) pleat allowance. For the front skirt panel, measure the distance between the front corner points. Cut a piece of fabric to the same length by the width measurement plus a 4 cm (1½ in) seam allowance and a 16 cm (6½ in) pleat allowance. Machine stitch the side edges, to join the skirt panels. Press and pin a 1 cm (½ in) wide double hem on both side edges and a 5 cm (2 in) wide double hem on the bottom edge. Herringbone stitch the hems.

2 To make the inverted pleats at each corner, make a pleat 4 cm (1½ in) in the front panel and 4 cm (1½ in) from the seam. Press towards the side panel. Fold another pleat in the side panel 4 cm (1½ in) wide and 12 cm (4¾ in) from the seam and press to the folded edge of the first pleat. Tack (baste) the pleats in place.

3 To join the skirt to the top piece, assemble the top and skirt pieces right sides together, matching up the centre of the pleat to the corner points. Pin and machine stitch the seam.

4 Cut four pieces of ribbon 15 cm (6 in) long. Position and pin the ends to either side of the struts of the chair back, on the underside piece. Pin underside and top pieces right sides together.

5 Machine stitch the seam, leaving a 20 cm (8 in) gap at the back. Turn the cushion right sides out. Sew the zip (zipper) to the opening edges. Insert the pad.

6 Make a template of the backrest. Use to cut four pieces of wadding (batting) and assemble. Zigzag stitch the edges. Cut two calico (cotton) pieces to the same size, plus a 2 cm (¾ in) allowance. Right sides together, machine stitch the seam, leaving a 15 cm (6 in) gap. Turn right sides out and insert pad. Turn opening edges under and slip stitch gap closed. Cut two pieces of fabric to match template, plus a 2 cm (¾ in) allowance. Cut ribbons 20 cm (8 in) long. Pin each pair on either side of top piece. Assemble right sides together and machine stitch seam, leaving a gap of 15 cm (6 in). Turn right sides out. Turn edges under and slip stitch the gap closed.

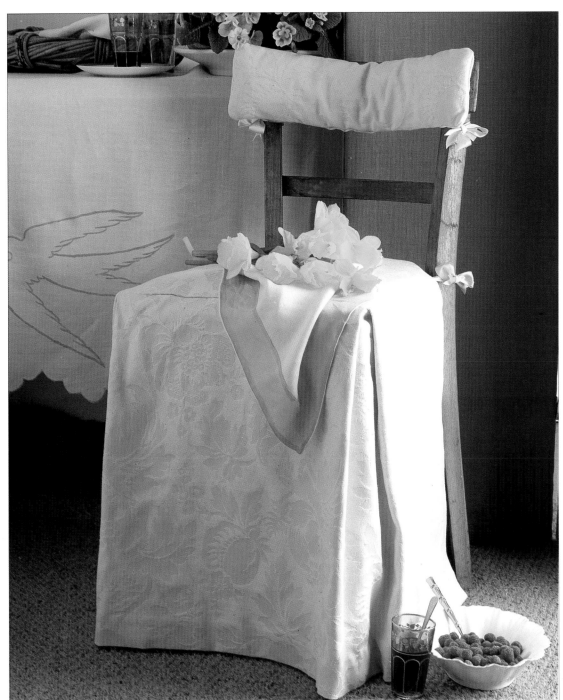

Lined and Headed Curtains

Ready-made heading tapes are available in gathered and pleated styles and are easily applied to the fabric. Gathers and pleats are formed by pulling up the drawstrings.

YOU WILL NEED

MATERIALS
fabric
matching thread
curtain weights
lining
tacking (basting) thread
heading tape
cardboard or cord tidy

EQUIPMENT
tape measure
scissors
pins
needles
iron
fabric marker
sewing machine

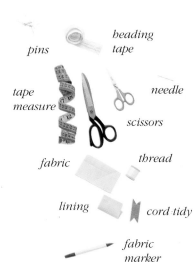

pins   *heading tape*

tape measure   *needle*

scissors

fabric   *thread*

lining   *cord tidy*

fabric marker

TO MAKE AND LINE THE CURTAIN

1 Measure the width of the track or pole. Measure the length that the curtain is intended to cover. Cut the main fabric to one and a half times the width measurement by the length measurement, the width of the tape plus 2 cm (¾ in) turning allowance and 10 cm (4 in) hem allowance. Join the fabric lengths, if necessary. Turn and press a 4 cm (1½ in) wide single hem along the side edge and a 5 cm (2 in) hem along the bottom edge. Mitre the corners and insert curtain weights. Herringbone stitch the hem. Cut the lining 14 cm (5¾ in) shorter than the curtain-fabric length and 8 cm (3¼ in) less than the curtain-fabric width. Turn and press a 1.5 cm (⅝ in) wide hem all round the side edges.

2 On the wrong side of the curtain fabric, mark the central line. Mark parallel lines 30 cm (12 in) apart across the curtain. Pin the curtain and lining together down the central line. Fold the lining back over the pins and lock stitch the fabrics together.

3 Repeat step 2 at each marked line, working outwards to the side edges. Tack (baste) the top edge of the fabric to the lining. Slip stitch the lining fabric to the curtain fabric all around the side and bottom hems.

TO APPLY HEADING TAPE

1 Turn and press the top edge of the curtain to the wrong side by 2 cm (¾ in). Turn and press the folded edges again by the width of the tape. Pin and tack (baste) the heading tape in place, matching up the top edges of the curtain and tape.

2 Machine stitch the tape to the fabric along the top and bottom and the leading edge (that is, the edge that is pulled across the window). Pull up the free ends of the drawstrings, to gather up the tape to form pleats.

3 At the required width, wind the drawstrings around a piece of cardboard or a cord-tidy. Secure the cardboard or cord-tidy to the back of the curtain with a few stitches. Before drycleaning, undo the drawstrings so that the curtain lies flat.

Curtain with Fabric Ties

Define a curtain heading with contrasting fabric
and delicate ties.

YOU WILL NEED

MATERIALS
fabric
matching threads
contrasting fabric

EQUIPMENT
tape measure
scissors
iron
sewing machine
needles
pins

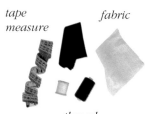

*tape
measure*

fabric

thread

pins

scissors

needle

1 Measure the width of the track or
pole and the length the curtain is
intended to cover. Cut the main fabric
to one and a half times the width by
the length, plus a 5 cm (2 in) turning
allowance and a 10 cm (4 in) hem
allowance. Turn and press a 1 cm (½ in)
wide double hem along both side
edges, and a 5 cm (2 in) double hem
along the bottom edge. Machine stitch
the hems. On the top edge, turn and
press a 5 cm (2 in) wide single hem.

2 Calculate the number of ties
required for the top edge of the
curtain, spacing them 20 cm (8 in)
apart. For each tie, cut a piece of contrasting fabric measuring 6 x 40 cm
(2¼ x 16 in). Fold in half lengthways,
right sides together. Stitch along the
length. Press the seam to the centre
and stitch across one width. Trim and
turn the tie right sides out. Tuck in
the raw edges and slip stitch across
the width.

3 Fold the ties in half widthways, and
position and pin the folded end to the
right side, top edge of the main fabric,
20 cm (8 in) apart. Machine stitch in
place.

4 To make the heading, cut a piece of
contrasting fabric to the width of the
main fabric by 12 cm (4¾ in). Fold and
press a 2 cm (¾ in) turning all round the
heading piece.

5 Position and pin the heading to the
top edge of the curtain, matching up
the fold edges. Machine stitch all round
the heading.

6 On either side of each tie, pin a
1 cm (½ in) wide tuck (pleat), 8 cm
(3¼ in) long, to the right-side of the
curtain. Machine stitch the tucks
(pleats).

Mosquito-net Bed Drapes

This exotic canopy is suspended from the ceiling;
cut the length generously so that it drapes.

YOU WILL NEED

MATERIALS
7 m (23 ft) muslin or sheer
    fabric
matching thread
ribbon
flexible plastic boning
invisible thread
large hoop, about 60 cm (24 in)
    diameter

EQUIPMENT
tape measure
scissors
sewing machine
needle
sticky tape
pins

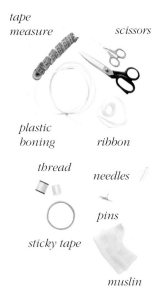

*tape
measure*   *scissors*

*plastic
boning*   *ribbon*

thread
        needles

        pins
sticky tape

        muslin

1 Measure the fall of the canopy to the floor and add a 30 cm (12 in) allowance. To decide the width of the curtain, measure the width of the bed and add three-quarters of the length of the bed on both sides. Join three lengths of fabric to make up the width; use French seams. Turn and press a double hem on both sides and machine stitch the hems.

4 Turn the work right sides out. Across the top, turn under and press a double hem of 1 cm (½ in). Machine stitch. Run two rows of gathering stitches along this hem. Cut an 8 cm (3¼ in) length of ribbon, and insert it into the hem. Slip stitch it in place.

2 Match up the hems and stitch a seam, 75 cm (29 in) in length, from the top, making a tube.

5 Make a ring with the boning and secure in place with sticky tape. Cut four lengths of invisible thread about 1 m (1 yard) long. Fold each thread in half and tie the folded end at four equal intervals around the boning ring. Use sticky tape to hold the threads in position. Tie the loose ends together. Holding the knotted threads, slip the ring under the canopy and stitch the knot to the gathered hem, under the tape.

3 Lay the canopy out flat, with wrong sides together and with the opening centred. Level with the opening, mark a diagonal line from either side to within 10 cm (4 in) of the centre seam. Turn it wrong sides out and stitch a French seam on the marked line.

6 Suspend the canopy from the ceiling with a length of invisible thread. Trim away any excess fabric from the bottom hem. Turn and press a 1 cm (½ in) wide double hem. Pin and machine stitch in place.

Café-style Curtain

An attractive, eye-catching curtain that hangs over the lower half of a window, with a scalloped heading and simple fabric loops.

YOU WILL NEED

MATERIALS
fabric
facing fabric
matching thread
graph paper
card (cardboard)

EQUIPMENT
tape measure
scissors
sewing machine
pins
iron
fabric marker
needle

tape measure

*card
(cardboard)*

scissors

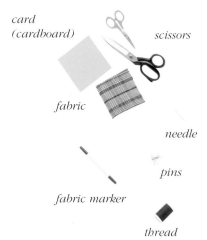

fabric

needle

pins

fabric marker

thread

1 Measure the length of the pole. Cut one width of fabric to this measurement, plus an 8 cm (3¼ in) hem allowance, by the length of the drop from the pole to the window sill, plus a 10 cm (4 in) hem allowance and 10 cm (4 in) extra for the fabric loops. Join widths together if necessary. Cut facing fabric to the same width by 40 cm (16 in) long. On the facing, press and turn under a hem of 6 mm (5⁄16 in). Machine stitch. Assemble the curtain and facing right sides together, top edges matching, and pin them. Cut out a card (cardboard) scallop template (pattern) (see page 22) to your required size.

2 Divide the finished curtain width by the width of the scallop 12 cm (4¾ in) and the strips in between - these should be 4–7 cm (1½–2¾ in) wide - to calculate the number of scallops required. The curtain should have a strip at each end. Placing the top of the template (pattern) at the top of the curtain, mark around the template with a fabric marker. Work across the curtain, spacing the scallops a strip-width apart.

3 Machine stitch the facing to the curtain along the marked line. Trim to 1 cm (½ in) from the stitching and clip the corners and into the curves.

4 Turn the work right sides out. Top stitch across the top, 4 mm (3⁄16 in) from the edge.

5 Turn and press a double hem of 2 cm (¾ in) along each side of the curtain. Turn and press a double hem of 5 cm (2 in) at the bottom of the curtain. Mitre the corners and machine stitch or slip stitch the hem in place. Turn and press under a single hem of 4 cm (1½ in) on both sides of the facing. Slip stitch the facing and all hems in place.

6 To make fabric loops, turn the strip to the wrong side by 5 cm (2 in) and pin and machine stitch to the facing.

Shower Curtain

Make a practical, waterproof curtain from boldly patterned PVC (vinyl), featuring an eyelet heading. An eyelet kit can be bought inexpensively from department stores.

YOU WILL NEED

MATERIALS
PVC (vinyl)
matching thread
eyelet kit

EQUIPMENT
tape measure
scissors
sewing machine
pencil
hammer

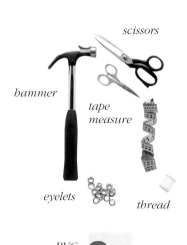

scissors

hammer

tape measure

eyelets　*thread*

PVC (vinyl)

pencil

1 Measure the fall from rail (rod) to floor. Cut PVC (vinyl) to this length, plus 4 cm (1½ in) hem and 10 cm (4 in) heading allowances. Cut width to length and a half of shower rail. On top edge, machine stitch a 5 cm (2 in) wide hem in place. Machine stitch side and bottom hems 4 cm (1½ in).

2 Mark the position of the eyelets about 20 cm (8 in) apart. Separate the two halves of the eyelet. Using the assembling tool, place the end over the marked point, with the plastic disc underneath. Tap sharply with a hammer to pierce the fabric.

3 Turn the plastic disc over, place the raised eyelet on the disc, lay the hem over and push the eyelet through the pierced hole.

4 Press the other eyelet-half open side down on to the raised part and position the other end of the assembling tool over the eyelet. Tap sharply two or three times with a hammer. Fold a 5 cm (2 in) wide double hem on bottom edge. Machine stitch in place.

Slot-headed Sheer Curtain

Mainly used for nets or sheer fabrics, this type of curtain heading may also be suitable for some lightweight fabrics.

YOU WILL NEED

MATERIALS
sheer fabric
matching thread
chain weight
plastic-covered wire
hooks

EQUIPMENT
tape measure
scissors
sewing machine
iron
pins
needles

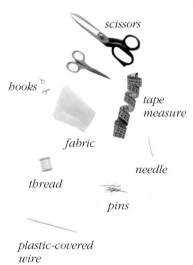

scissors

hooks

tape measure

fabric

needle

thread

pins

plastic-covered wire

1 Measure the width of the window by the length that the curtain is intended to cover. Cut the fabric width to three times the width measurement. Add a 10 cm (4 in) heading and a 10 cm (4 in) hem allowance to the length measurement. Fabric widths should be joined with French seams. Turn and press a 1.5 cm (⅝ in) wide double hem along each side edge. Machine stitch the hems.

2 Turn and press a 5 cm (2 in) wide double hem on the top edge. Pin and machine stitch. Stitch a parallel line 2.5 cm (1 in) above the stitching line.

3 At the bottom edge of the curtain, turn and press a 5 cm (2 in) wide double hem. Slip stitch a chain weight into the fold of the hem. Pin and machine stitch.

4 Feed the wire through the slot, gathering the net up. Screw the hooks into the window frame and attach the hooks to the wire.

Draped Curtains

Fix a curtain pole above the window and hang sheer curtains with casings and a draped central panel for a simple elegant look.

YOU WILL NEED

MATERIALS
fabric
matching thread
paper

EQUIPMENT
tape measure
scissors
iron
sewing machine
ruler
pencil
needles
pins

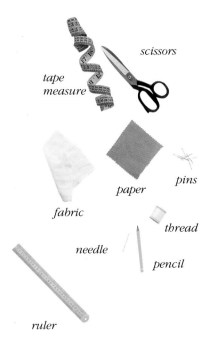

scissors

tape measure

paper

pins

fabric

needle

thread

pencil

ruler

1 Measure the length from the pole to the floor, adding a 30 cm (12 in) allowance. The width of the curtain will depend on how much fullness is required. Cut two curtain widths to size. Turn and press a double hem 1 cm (½ in) wide along the side edges. Machine stitch the hem.

2 Make a paper pattern in the shape of a trapezoid, for the draped section. The top edge of the shape should be the desired width between the curtains plus 50 cm (20 in); the bottom edge should be the width of both curtain widths plus 50 cm (20 in). The height of the shape should be the width of one curtain plus 30 cm (12 in).

3 Cut the fabric to size, turn and press a double hem 1 cm (½ in) wide on the top and bottom edges. Machine stitch the hems. Run a gathering stitch along the raw side edges.

4 Align the top edge of one curtain length to the gathered side edge of the central panel. Align wrong side of curtain lengths to right side of central panel. Distribute gathers along the length. Pin and machine stitch the seam.

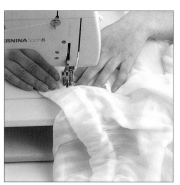

5 Make the pole casings in the top edge of the curtain widths. Pin a pleat the width of the pole circumference plus a 2 cm (¾ in) seam allowance to the wrong side of the curtain width. Machine stitch the seam.

6 Thread the pole through the casings. Fold the central draped section over the pole to the front.

Painted Roller-blind

A roller-blind kit contains all the parts you need to make a blind: a wooden roller, the brackets, tacks, lath and cord pull. The fabric should be treated with a stiffening spray.

YOU WILL NEED

MATERIALS
roller-blind kit
fabric
paper
graph paper
fabric paint
fabric stiffener spray
tacks
matching thread

EQUIPMENT
tape measure
saw
scissors
pencil
fabric marker
paintbrush
iron
hammer
pins
sewing machine
screwdriver

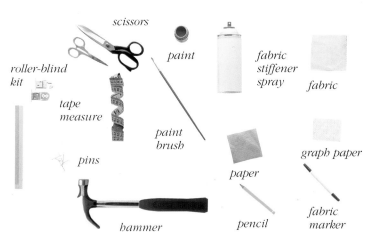

scissors

paint

fabric stiffener spray

fabric

roller-blind kit

tape measure

paint brush

pins

paper

graph paper

hammer

pencil

fabric marker

1 Measure the width of the window. Cut the roller to size and fix the brackets and roller in place. Measure the width of the roller and the length of the window. Cut one piece of fabric to this size, plus a 30 cm (12 in) allowance to the length. Scale up the template from pages 20–1. Lay the template (pattern) on the fabric and draw all round it with a fabric marker.

2 Using a paintbrush, apply the fabric paint to the cloth, tracing the design. To fix the fabric paint, press on the wrong side, according to the manufacturer's instructions.

4 To make the lath casing, turn and press to the wrong side a double hem of 4 cm (1½ in). Machine stitch the hem. Cut the lath to size and insert it in the casing. Machine stitch across each end.

3 Hang the fabric in a well aired (ventilated) room. Spray the fabric with the stiffener spray, as per the manufacturer's instructions. Place the fabric face-up, and lay the roller across the fabric 4 cm (1½ in) from the top edge, with the adhesive strip face-up. Pull the fabric edge over and press it firmly to the adhesive strip. Hammer tacks in place at 2 cm (¾ in) intervals, with one at each end. Roll up the blind.

5 Screw the cord holder to the centre of the lath.

Loop-headed Curtain

Choose contrasting fabrics to make this simple
yet effective curtain.

YOU WILL NEED

MATERIALS
curtain fabric
facing fabric
contrasting fabric
matching threads
tacking (basting) thread

EQUIPMENT
tape measure
scissors
iron
sewing machine
pins

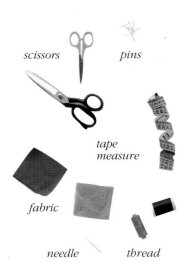

scissors *pins*

tape measure

fabric

needle *thread*

1 Measure the width of the pole and the length of drop. Cut one piece of fabric to the width, plus an 8 cm (3¼ in) hem and a 30 cm (12 in) fullness allowance, by the length plus a 2 cm (¾ in) seam and a 10 cm (4 in) hem allowance. Cut facing to same width by 10 cm (4 in) depth. Turn and press a 6 mm (³⁄₁₆ in) wide hem on the bottom edge of the facing.

2 Calculate the number of loops for the top edge of curtain, spacing them 20 cm (8 in) apart. For each loop, cut a piece of contrasting fabric 30 × 14 cm (12 × 5½ in). Fold in half lengthways, right sides together, and stitch along the length. Turn right sides out and press the seam to the centre of the tie.

3 Fold in half widthways. Pin and tack the raw edges of the loop to the top edge of the curtain. With right sides together and top edges matching, pin the facing to the curtain fabric. Machine stitch the seam.

4 Turn and press a 2 cm (¾ in) wide double hem along the side edges and a 5 cm (2 in) wide double hem along the bottom edge. Fold the facing to the wrong side and slip stitch the facing to the main fabric, at the side seams. Top stitch 4 mm (³⁄₁₆ in) from the top edge.

Simple Shaped Valance

A valance will give a decorative finish to curtain tops and conceal tracks.

YOU WILL NEED

MATERIALS
graph paper
paper
adhesive-coated stiffener
fabric
glue
Velcro touch spots or
  decorative tacks

EQUIPMENT
tape measure
pencil
scissors

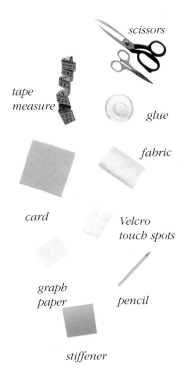

scissors

tape measure

glue

fabric

card

Velcro touch spots

graph paper

pencil

stiffener

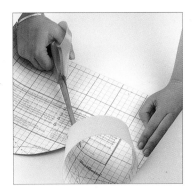

1 To width of window add 3 cm (1¼ in) to fix valance to frame, 10 cm (4 in) to fix it to the wall. Scale up the scallop template (pattern) on page 22 to size. Cut out a paper template (pattern). Cut a piece of adhesive-coated stiffener to the width and length desired. Cut a piece of fabric to size plus a 2 cm (¾ in) allowance all round. Lay template (pattern) on the wrong side of stiffener; draw round it and trim.

2 Lay the fabric face-down on a table and peel away the paper backing from one side of the stiffener. Press the fusible side face-down on the wrong side of the fabric and smooth it in place.

3 Trim away the excess fabric, leaving a 2 cm (¾ in) turning allowance all round. Clip into the curves. Spread a line of glue on the wrong side of the stiffener. Fold the turning allowance over the stiffener edge and press it in place.

4 To the top and side edges of the valance, glue one half of the Velcro touch spots. Glue the other half to the top side edges above and to each side of the window.

Bow-trimmed Tie-back

An attractive and practical feature in a window-dressing scheme; bow trimmings could also be used to embellish cushions and covers.

YOU WILL NEED

MATERIALS
fabric
matching thread
iron-on interfacing
2 brass rings

EQUIPMENT
tape measure
scissors
iron
pins
sewing machine
needle

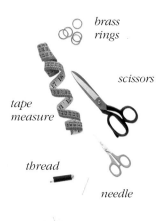

brass rings

scissors

tape measure

thread

needle

pins

fabric

interfacing

1 Gather back the curtain and measure the distance from the tie-back hook around the curtain and back.

4 For the bow, cut a piece of fabric 60 x 14 cm (24 x 5¾ in). Fold in half lengthways, right sides together. Pin and stitch the long edge; leave a gap of 15 cm (6 in). Press seam to centre. Stitch short edges. Turn right sides out and press. Turn in opening edges, press and slip stitch the gap closed. Cut one piece of fabric 12 x 12 cm (4¾ x 4¾ in). Fold it in half, right sides together, and stitch the longest edge. Turn right sides out. Press the seam to the centre.

2 Cut two pieces of interfacing and two pieces of fabric to this length, by 12 cm (4¾ in) width, plus 2 cm (¾ in) seam allowance all round. Using a hot iron, press the fusible side of the interfacing to the wrong sides of the fabric. Assemble with right sides together. Pin and machine stitch the seam, leaving a gap of 10 cm (4 in) on a length seam. Clip the corners.

5 Tie the longest strip into a bow, ensuring folds and ends are even; pin in place.

3 Turn right sides out. Press and turn in the opening edges; slip stitch the gap closed. On the underside of the tie-back, stitch a brass ring centrally to each end.

6 Pin the bow to the front of the tie-back. Fold the smaller strip over the centre of the bow and the tie-back and turn in the raw edges. Slip stitch the ends together.

Tassel

Shop-bought tassels can be expensive and choice is restricted. Make your own; attached to cords they make attractive bell-pulls or curtain tie-backs. Gathered at the top, they can be stitched singly to the corners of cushions, throws or tablecloths. You will need about six skeins of embroidery thread for a curtain tie-back tassel and two for a cushion tassel.

YOU WILL NEED

MATERIALS
cardboard
embroidery thread
thread
cord
sticky tape
gold thread

EQUIPMENT
tape measure
scissors
needles

scissors

embroidery thread

thread

tape measure

sticky tape

card

needle

cord

1 Cut two pieces of cardboard 20 cm (8 in) by the desired length of the tassel. Fold them in half lengthways. Wind the embroidery thread around the card neatly, to the thickness required.

2 Thread a needle and work a chain stitch across the top. For a simpler tassel, just tie a loop around the top and pull up tightly.

3 Make a loop in a length of cord about 40 cm (16 in) long and tie a knot. Trim the ends and secure with sticky tape. Cut the tassel threads from the card.

4 Wrap the tassel around the knot, and stitch the top of the tassel to the cord above the knot.

5 Bind the strands of the tassel together below the knot, with gold thread.

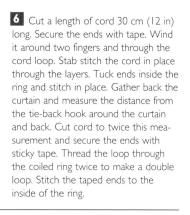

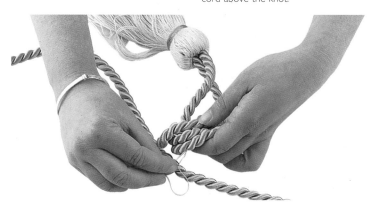

6 Cut a length of cord 30 cm (12 in) long. Secure the ends with tape. Wind it around two fingers and through the cord loop. Stab stitch the cord in place through the layers. Tuck ends inside the ring and stitch in place. Gather back the curtain and measure the distance from the tie-back hook around the curtain and back. Cut cord to twice this measurement and secure the ends with sticky tape. Thread the loop through the coiled ring twice to make a double loop. Stitch the taped ends to the inside of the ring.

Fabric-flowered Tie-back

Purchased fabric flowers are woven into a
rope tie-back.

YOU WILL NEED

MATERIALS
rope
matching thread
fabric flowers and leaves

EQUIPMENT
tape measure
scissors
needle

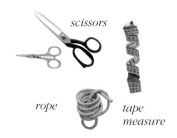

scissors

rope

tape measure

needle

fabric flowers and leaves

thread

1 Gather back the curtain at the height desired. Measure the distance from the tie-back hook, around the curtain and back. Cut a piece of rope to six times this measurement. Make a loop in one end and stitch the end in place.

2 At the length of the finished tie-back, make a second loop. Stitch it in place.

3 Wind the rope around the two loops and the length of the tie back. Firmly stab stitch it in place to secure. On the right side, insert the stems of the fabric flowers and leaves through the strands of rope.

4 Stitch them securely to the wrong side of the tie-back.

Piping-cord Trimmed Tie-back

Tie-backs should be made once the curtains are in place.

YOU WILL NEED

MATERIALS
paper
heavy interfacing
fabric
tacking (basting) thread
piping cord
matching thread
brass rings

EQUIPMENT
tape measure
scissors
pencil
iron
pins
needle
sewing machine

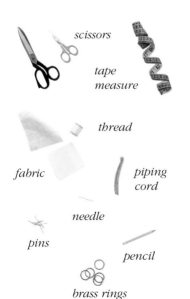

1 Gather back curtain and measure the distance from tie-back hook, around the curtain and back. Make a template (pattern)15 cm (6 in) wide and required length. Fold in half and draw a half-crescent shape with rounded ends 7 cm (2 in). Cut out template and use it to cut fabric and interfacing. Press interfacing to wrong side of fabric.

2 With right sides facing, pin and tack (baste) the cord all round the top fabric piece. Start at an unobtrusive place and tuck the ends into the seam allowance. Machine stitch the piping cord in place, using a zipper foot. Cut into the curves.

3 Pin the top and underside fabrics right sides together. Machine stitch the seam, leaving a gap of 10 cm (4 in) on a straight side. Clip into curves and turn them right sides out. Turn in opening edges and slip stitch the gap closed.

4 On the underside of the tie-back, stitch a brass ring centrally to each end.

Quilt

Choose satin or a patterned fabric for the upper side of this updated version of a traditional quilt. It is worked in four quarters, to make it more manageable; the upperside fabric and ticking are joined once the design is complete.

YOU WILL NEED

MATERIALS
ticking, or other tightly woven
  lining fabric
wadding (batting)
upper fabric
tacking (basting) thread
white and matching thread

EQUIPMENT
tape measure
scissors
pins
needle
fabric marker
sewing machine
iron

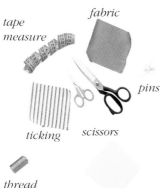

tape measure

fabric

pins

ticking *scissors*

thread

wadding

fabric marker

2 Using the ticking stripes as a guide, tack (baste) parallel lines from the centre to the outer edges, through the three layers, in both directions.

5 Stitch a border 1 cm (½ in) wide all round the outer edges of quilted panel.

3 On the upperside, mark out squares approximately 30 cm (12 in) square with a fabric marker, using the tacking (basting) as a guide. With thread matching the upperside fabric in the bobbin, and thread in the top of the sewing machine, work a straight stitch along the marked lines.

1 Calculate the required width and length of the finished bedcover. Divide these measurements by two to give the measurements required for each panel. Cut four pieces each of ticking, wadding (batting) and upper fabric to this size, plus 2 cm (¾ in) all round. Assemble the wadding (batting) between the ticking and the upper fabric, right-sides out. Smooth out. Pin layers together, starting from the centre and working outwards. Repeat with other three sections.

4 To join the four pieces, trim the wadding (batting) back to stitching line. Trim the ticking and upperside fabric back to 2 cm (¾ in) from stitching line. With right sides together, stitch upper-side fabrics, leaving an allowance of 1.5 cm (⅝ in). Turn both edges of ticking under by 1.5 cm (⅝ in). Press and ladder stitch them together.

6 To finish the outer edges, trim wadding (batting) back to stitching line. Trim the ticking and upperside fabric to 2 cm (¾ in) from the stitching line. Turn under a hem of 1 cm (½ in) press it and slip stitch the edges together.

Bedcover

A fitted bedcover with a skirt is easy to make and ideal for a bed more often used as seating.

YOU WILL NEED

MATERIALS
fabric
piping cord
contrasting fabric
tacking (basting) thread
thread
bias binding

EQUIPMENT
tape measure
pinking shears
sewing machine
pins
scissors
needle
iron

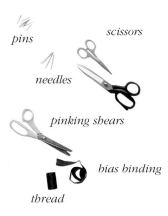

pins *scissors*

needles

pinking shears

bias binding

thread

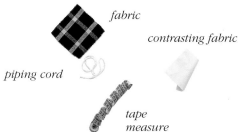

fabric

contrasting fabric

piping cord

tape measure

1 For the top panel, measure the width and length of the bed, with the blankets on. With pinking shears, cut the fabric to this size plus a 2 cm (¾ in) seam allowance all round. For the side panels, measure the depth of the mattress. Cut two side panels to the length by the depth, plus a 2 cm (¾ in) seam allowance all round. Cut one end panel to the width of the mattress by the depth plus a 2 cm (¾ in) seam allowance all round. To make the skirt, measure the fall from the bottom of the mattress to the floor. Cut two pieces of fabric to this depth, plus 4 cm (1½ in) by the length of the bed, plus a 34 cm (13½ in) pleat allowance. Cut one piece to the width of the bed, plus 24 cm (9½ in). Cover the piping cord with the contrasting fabric.

2 Mark curves at both corners of the top panel. Starting at the top edge of the panel, pin the piping cord all around the panel with the raw edges of the contrasting fabric facing the edge of the panel. Tack (baste) it in place.

3 Stitch the side panels and end panel together by the shortest edges. Press the seams open. With right sides together, pin the side panels to the top panel, matching the seams to the centre of the curves. Machine stitch seams.

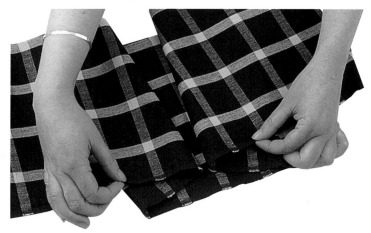

4 To make the skirt, stitch the three panels together along the shortest edges. With the side panels right sides facing, make a pleat (tuck) 10 cm (4 in) from the end of the width piece. Fold another pleat (tuck) of 10 cm (4 in) on the length piece, matching to the folded edges, to make an inverted pleat (tuck). Press the pleats (tucks) and tack (baste) them in place. Repeat at the other corner.

5 With right sides together, match the corners of the side panels to the centres of the pleats. Machine stitch the side panels to the skirt.

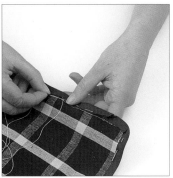

6 Trim the hem and top edge of the top panel all round with bias binding.

Pieced Throw

This luxurious throw can be made from recycled scraps from old clothes or furnishings. Velvet patches cut from old clothes, dyed and pressed to resemble an antique patchwork, have been used here.

YOU WILL NEED

MATERIALS
cardboard
velvet
tacking (basting) thread
thread
lining fabric

EQUIPMENT
tape measure
scissors
pinking shears
pins
needle

tape measure   *scissors*

cardboard

thread   *fabric*

pins

pinking shears

needle

tacking (basting) thread

1 Measure the desired width and length of the finished bedcover and calculate the number of patches required with a length of 20 cm (8 in) and width of 10 cm (4 in). Draw and cut out a patch template (pattern) in cardboard. Draw around the template on the wrong side of the fabric and cut out the shapes with pinking shears.

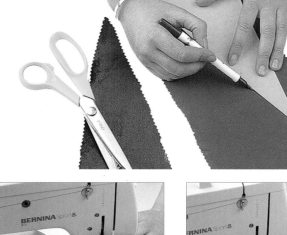

2 To join triangular shapes, pin and tack (baste) right sides together along the diagonal edge to make rectangles, leaving a 6 mm (¼ in) seam allowance.

3 Machine stitch the seam and press it open.

4 Pin, tack (baste) and machine stitch the rectangles together along the longest edge to form strips. Press the seams open.

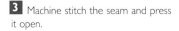

5 Pin, tack (baste) and machine stitch the strips together.

6 Cut one piece of lining to the size of the patchwork panel. With right sides together, pin and stitch the panel and lining together all around, leaving a 6 mm (¼ in) seam allowance and an opening of 50 cm (20 in). Turn the throw right side out, through the gap. Turn the raw edges under 6 mm (¼ in) and press. Slip stitch the gap closed.

Bordered Throw

Emphasize the quality of an unusual fabric with a border; contrasting colours and textiles will define the area like a frame.

YOU WILL NEED

MATERIALS
upper fabric
lining fabric
matching thread

EQUIPMENT
scissors
tape measure
pins
sewing machine
iron
needle

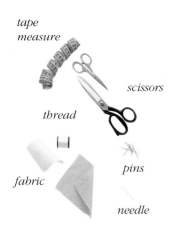

tape measure

scissors

thread

fabric

pins

needle

1 Cut the upper fabric to the size of the finished throw, less 8 cm (3¼ in) all round. Lining fabric should be same size plus a 12 cm (5 in) allowance all around. Assemble the lining and upper fabric right sides together. Pin and stitch seam, starting and finishing 2 cm (¾ in) from each edge of upper fabric. Match two bottom edges and stitch in the same way.

2 Centre the upper fabric lengthways, to create a loose top and bottom border 10 cm (4 in) wide. Press the seams open. Fold and pin the side edges of the lining and upper fabric.

3 Machine stitch or hand stitch the seam, starting 2 cm (¾ in) from the edge of the upper fabric and finish 2 cm (¾ in) from the end. Repeat on the other side but leave an 80 cm (32 in) gap. Press the seams open. Turn right sides out.

4 Turn in the opening edges and press them. Slip stitch the gap closed. Press in a border of 10 cm (4 in) all around. At the corners, tuck the excess fabric under so that a diagonal seam is formed. Press and ladder stitch or slip stitch the folded edges together.

Pillowcase with Ties

This type of pillowcase can also be made up to cover scatter cushions.

YOU WILL NEED

MATERIALS
pillow
fabric
thread

EQUIPMENT
tape measure
scissors
sewing machine
pins
needle
iron

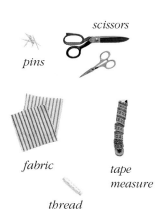

scissors

pins

fabric

tape measure

thread

1 Cut one piece of fabric twice the pillow length by the width plus a 4 cm (1½ in) seam allowance. For the facings, cut two pieces of fabric 6 cm (2½ in) wide by the pillow width plus a 4 cm (1½ in) seam allowance. Turn, press and stitch a hem of 6 mm (⅜ in) on one long side of both facings. With right sides together, stitch the facings together along the short edges. Fold the pillowcase in half lengthways and stitch the side seams.

2 For the ties, cut six pieces of fabric 15 × 8 cm (6 × 3 in). Fold the strips in half lengthways, with right sides together, and machine stitch along one side and down the length. Turn the strips right side out.

3 On the right side, position and pin the ties in three pairs, at equal distances. Tack (baste) them in place. With right sides together, pin the facings to the pillowcase piece. Stitch them in place.

4 Turn the facing to the wrong side and press it. Pin, tack (baste) and top stitch around the edge.

Self-bordered Duvet Cover

Make matching self-bordered pillowcases and duvet covers, with contrasting stitching.

YOU WILL NEED
(FOR BOTH DUVET COVER
AND PILLOWCASE)

MATERIALS
fabric
matching and contrasting thread
tacking (basting) thread
Velcro or large press-fasteners

EQUIPMENT
tape measure
quilt
scissors
pins
sewing machine
needle
iron
pillow

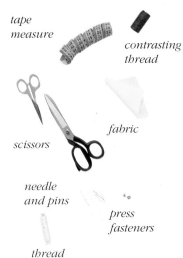

tape measure

contrasting thread

scissors

fabric

needle and pins

press fasteners

thread

1 Measure the dimensions of the quilt. For the top, cut one piece of fabric to the size of the quilt plus a 15 cm (6 in) overhang and seam allowance to the width; add 27 cm (11 in) to the length. Cut another piece to the size of the quilt, plus 15 cm (6 in) to the width and 10 cm (4 in) to the length. Fold and stitch a double hem of 2.5 cm (1 in) on both top edges. Assemble the two layers with right sides together. Fold over the underside hemmed edge to overlap the top hemmed edge. Stitch the seam across the two side edges and the bottom edge.

2 Turn the work right side out. Press the seams and tack (baste) a parallel line 3.5 cm (1⅜ in) from the folded edge all round. Work a close machine zigzag stitch all round over the tacking (basting) in the contrasting-colour thread.

3 Position the press-fasteners 20 cm (8 in) apart along the overlapping hems, ensuring each pair matches up. Stitch the fasteners. Top stitch an X-figure at each end of the closure. See page 21 for attaching the Velcro.

Self-bordered Pillowcase

1 Measure the dimensions of the pillow. For the top, cut one piece of fabric to the size of the pillow plus a 7 cm (2¾ in) seam and border allowance to the width and add a 47 cm (21 in) border, seam and pocket-flap allowance to the length. For the underside, cut one piece of fabric to the same width; add a 12 cm (5 in) hem, seam and border allowance to the length. On one width edge, turn, press and machine stitch a double hem of 2.5 cm (1in) on both pieces. Assemble and pin the top and underside pieces right sides together. Fold the top piece pocket-flap over the underside by 30 cm (12 in). Machine stitch the width and the two side seams.

 **2** Turn the work right side out and press the seams. Stitch a tacking (basting) line 5 cm (2 in) from the folded edge. Work a close machine zigzag stitch all round over the tacking (basting) in the contrasting-colour thread.

 **3** Work a close machine zigzag stitch 7 mm (⅜ in) from the folded edge all round.

Picot-edged and Ribbon-trimmed Pillowcases

Give self-bordered pillowcases one of these charming decorative treatments.

YOU WILL NEED

MATERIALS
cardboard
matching thread
self-bordered pillowcase
contrasting thread
4 cm (1½ in) wide ribbon

EQUIPMENT
scissors
fabric marker
sewing machine
tape measure
small sharp scissors
pins

cardboard

pins

scissors

tape measure

pillowcase

fabric marker

thread   *ribbon*

FOR THE PICOT-EDGED PILLOWCASE

1 Trace the outline of picot edging (page 22) on to cardboard and cut out template (pattern). Lay it on the border. Mark around the template with the fabric marker all round the border.

2 Machine stitch 2 mm (1⁄16 in) inside the marked line with matching thread.

3 Run a zigzag machine stitch along the marked line in contrasting colour. Trim away the excess fabric.

FOR THE RIBBON-TRIMMED PILLOWCASE

1 All round the border mark 4 cm (1½ in) wide slits alternately about 7 cm (2¾ in) and 4 cm (1½ in) apart, beginning and ending with the wider spacing.

2 On the marked line, cut slits through the top layer of fabric with small sharp scissors. Tuck a length of ribbon into one corner and pin.

3 Weave the ribbon through the slits and cut the ribbon, tucking it into the second corner. Pin in place. Work a zigzag machine stitch over the raw edges of the slits. Repeat on all sides.

Appliquéd Sheet and Pillowcase

A bold appliquéd design gives bed linen unique appeal. The shapes could be cut from patterned or checked fabrics.

YOU WILL NEED

MATERIALS
graph paper
Bondaweb
coloured or patterned fabric
ready-made sheet and
   pillowcase
matching thread

EQUIPMENT
pencil
scissors
tape measure
iron
pins
sewing machine

pillowcase

tape measure

pencil

scissors

thread

pins

fabric

graph paper

Bondaweb

1 Scale up the designs featured on page 23 on to graph paper to your desired size . Cut one piece of Bondaweb 25 x 25 cm (10 x 10 in). Lay the Bondaweb over the drawn designs, paper side facing, and trace the outlines.

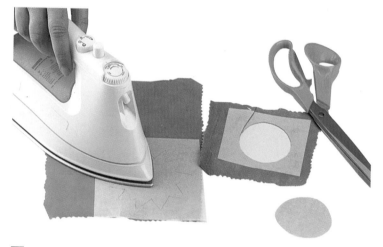

2 Cut four or five pieces of coloured or patterned fabric to about 20 x 20 cm (8 x 8 in). Cut roughly around the shapes. Using a hot iron, press the fusible side of the Bondaweb pieces, face-down, on the wrong side of the coloured or patterned fabrics. Cut out the shapes accurately.

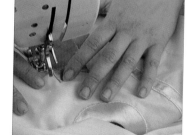

3 Peel away the paper backing from the Bondaweb. Arrange the cut-outs on the sheet and pillowcase, parallel to the fabric edge. Pin them in place. Using a hot iron, press over the cut-out pieces, removing the pins as you go.

4 Work a zigzag machine stitch all round the fused shapes.

Bordered Napkins

These two napkin projects feature stitched and fabric borders.

YOU WILL NEED

MATERIALS
fabric
contrasting thread
contrasting fabric
matching thread

EQUIPMENT
tape measure
scissors
iron
sewing machine

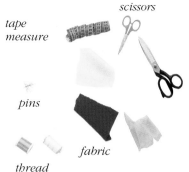

tape measure

scissors

pins

fabric

thread

needle

FOR THE STITCHED-BORDERED NAPKINS

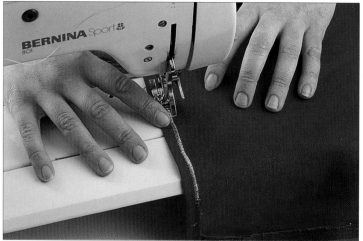

For each napkin, cut a piece of fabric 40 x 40 cm (16 x 16 in). Turn and press a 1 cm (½ in) hem to the right side. Mitre the corners. Work a close zigzag machine stitch in a contrasting colour over the raw edges all round.

FOR THE FABRIC-BORDER NAPKINS

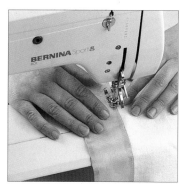

1 For each napkin, cut one piece of napkin fabric and one piece of contrasting fabric 40 x 40 cm (16 x 16 in). Right sides together, stitch all round the seam, leaving a 1 cm (½ in) seam allowance. Cut out the centre square of the contrasting fabric, leaving a 3 cm (1¼ in) border; clip the corners.

2 Turn through to the right side and press. Turn under and press the inner edge by 1 cm (½ in), snipping into the corners.

3 Top stitch 4 mm (³⁄₁₆ in) from the inside of the contrasting fabric all round. Top stitch 4 mm (³⁄₁₆ in) from the napkin edge all round.

Napkin Rings

Enhance your table setting with these napkin rings. Upholstery cord can be used in place of rope, for a more opulent look.

YOU WILL NEED

MATERIALS
rope
matching thread
fabric flowers
gold organza

EQUIPMENT
tape measure
scissors
needles

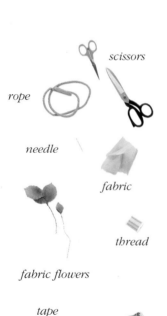

scissors

rope

needle

fabric

thread

fabric flowers

tape measure

1 Cut a length of rope 50 cm (20 in) long. Wind the rope around two fingers into a spiral. Stab stitch in place through the layers. Stitch the ends firmly in place.

2 Separate the bunches of fabric flowers. Trim the stems to 3 cm (1¼ in). Twist the stems together.

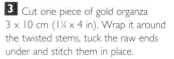

3 Cut one piece of gold organza 3 × 10 cm (1¼ × 4 in). Wrap it around the twisted stems, tuck the raw ends under and stitch them in place.

4 Stitch the bouquet firmly to the rope ring, concealing the rope ends.

Painted Tablecloth

Choose a fine white or cream linen, lawn or cambric for this delicate cloth. The birds are painted with water-based fabric paint and fixed by ironing; the cut-work is finished with a zigzag machine stitch, in contrasting thread.

YOU WILL NEED

MATERIALS
fabric (cotton or linen)
graph paper
stencil paper or card
fabric paint
cardboard
contrasting thread

EQUIPMENT
scissors
tape measure
pencil
marker pen
paintbrush
iron
fabric marker
sewing machine
small sharp scissors

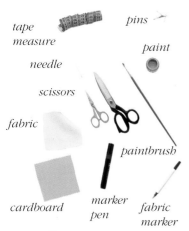

tape measure

pins

paint

needle

scissors

fabric

paintbrush

cardboard

marker pen

fabric marker

graph paper

1 Measure the table and depth of the hang. Cut the fabric accordingly, joining fabric widths if necessary. Trace the motif from page 23 on to graph paper; scale up to the desired size. Redraw with a marker pen.

2 Wash, dry and press the fabric. Mark out the position of the birds, spacing them at even intervals around the edge of the cloth. Position the bottom edge of the template (pattern) 10–15 cm (4–6 in) from the fabric edge. Slip the template (pattern) under the fabric and smooth out the fabric. Using a paintbrush, apply the fabric paint to the cloth, tracing the design.

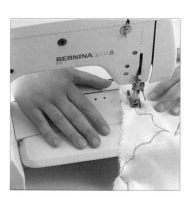

3 Fix the fabric paint by ironing on the wrong side of the fabric, according to the manufacturer's instructions.

4 Make a cardboard template (pattern) of the scallop shape on page 22. Draw around the template (pattern) along the edge of the cloth, with a fabric marker.

5 With contrasting thread, work a straight stitch along the marked line and then stitch a close zigzag machine stitch around the scallops. Trim the excess fabric down to the stitched edge, with small, sharp scissors.

Ribbon-trimmed Tablecloth

Add a splash of colour to a room; choose a boldly coloured fabric and trim it with a wide patterned or contrasting ribbon.

YOU WILL NEED

MATERIALS
fabric
thread
ribbon

EQUIPMENT
tape measure
scissors
iron
sewing machine
pins
needles

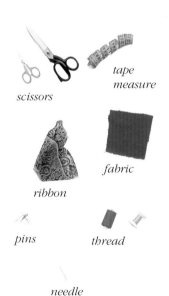

scissors

tape measure

fabric

ribbon

pins

thread

needle

1 Measure the length and width of the tabletop. Add the depth of the desired hang, plus a 3 cm (1½ in) hem allowance all round. Cut the fabric to these dimensions. Turn under and press a double hem of 1.5 cm (¾ in). Mitre the corners. Work a machine stitch all round the hem.

2 Starting in one corner, pin both edges of the ribbon parallel to the hem, making folds in the corners.

3 Work a zigzag machine stitch all round to attach the ribbon to the fabric.

4 In the corners, tuck the excess fabric under, so that a neat diagonal seam is formed. Slip stitch it in place.

Bedside Tablecloth

A tablecloth can be made of practically any type of fabric. A number of cloths can be layered on a table, the uppermost cloth falling short of the floor. To make a round cloth, lengths of fabric need to be joined.

YOU WILL NEED

MATERIALS
fabric
thread
fringing

EQUIPMENT
tape measure
scissors
sewing machine
drawing pin
string
pencil or fabric marker
iron
pins
needle

string

fabric

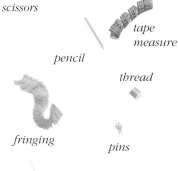

scissors

tape measure

pencil

thread

fringing

pins

needle

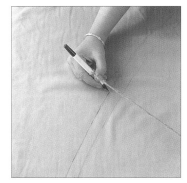

1 Measure the diameter of the table-top. Add to this twice the fall from tabletop to floor, plus a 3 cm (1½ in) hem allowance. Join fabric widths if necessary. Lay fabric on the floor and fold it in half lengthways. Push a drawing pin into the centre. Tie a piece of string the length of the radius to a pencil. Hold the other end to the pin and use it to draw a semicircle. Draw a second semi-circle 3 cm (1½ in) smaller than the first, to mark seam allowance.

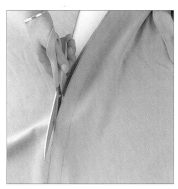

2 Cut carefully through both layers.

3 Fold in a single hem, matching the raw edges to the marked line; fold again and press. Fold the hem on the marked line, forming small pleats, and pin it flat.

4 Slip stitch the hem. Pin the fringe to the right side and machine stitch in place. Repeat the process with a contrasting cloth falling short of the floor. Finish this cloth with a fringe.

Kitchen Tablecloth and Napkins

A fringed edge works best with woven, checked
or tartan (plaid) fabrics that are loosely woven.

YOU WILL NEED

MATERIALS
fabric
matching thread

EQUIPMENT
tape measure
scissors
sewing machine
iron

scissors

fabric

tape measure

thread

pins

1 Measure the width and length of the tabletop. To these measurements, add twice the depth of the desired drop and the fringing allowance all round. Cut the fabric to this size, joining fabric widths with open seams if necessary.

2 Work a zigzag machine stitch all round at the desired depth of the fringe from the fabric edge.

3 Working one side at a time and starting from the outer edge, carefully separate and remove threads from the raw edges; pull away threads up to the zigzag stitched line.

4 For each napkin, cut a piece of fabric 40 × 40 cm (16 ×16 in). Repeat steps 2 and 3. Pick up two sections of the fringe and tie a small knot next to the edge of the cloth. Repeat all the way round.

CRAFT TIP
A needle can be used to separate the strands before pulling away.

Fabric-covered Screen

Re-cover an old screen or room divider; remove the old fabric and interlinings and sand the wood down. Use staples or decorative tacks to hold the new fabric in place; you can cover the staples with decorative braid around the edges. Cover each panel separately. Choose two different fabrics for each side of the screen, to create alternative looks.

YOU WILL NEED

MATERIALS
wooden frame screen
fabric
interlining
contrasting fabric
staples or tacks
braid
fabric glue
tape

EQUIPMENT
tape measure
scissors
staple gun
pins

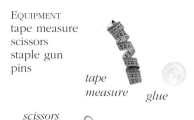

tape measure

glue

scissors

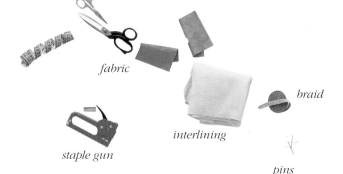

fabric

braid

interlining

staple gun

pins

1 Measure the length and width of each screen panel. For each panel cut a piece each of fabric, contrasting fabric and interlining to the size of the panel, plus a 3 cm (1¼ in) turning allowance all round, keeping the edges parallel to the selvedges. Lay the screen on a flat surface; cover one side of a panel with interlining. Staple or tack interlining to the frame working from the middle outwards .

4 Turn the screen over and repeat steps 1 and 2 with the contrasting fabric. Pin the second fabric to the first, stretching the fabric taut at each edge. Turn under a hem of 6 mm (⁵/₁₆ in), overlapping the raw edges of the first fabric and staple or tack it in place.

2 Staple or tack the interlining to the middle of the panel's bottom edge, and then to the middle of each side edge, stretching the fabric taut at each edge. Work outwards towards the corners. Trim the interlining to the edge of the frame.

3 Staple or tack the fabric to the frame. Fold the fabric over the frame and staple it to the narrow edge, stapling in the middle of the top, and then the bottom and then on either side. Trim the fabric back to 3 mm (⅛ in) from the staples.

5 On each end panel, measure the side edge and top edge. Cut a length of braid to this size, plus a 6 cm (2¼ in) turning allowance. For each central panel, measure the top edge only. Cut a piece of braid to this size, plus a 3 cm (1¼ in) turning allowance. Apply a line of glue to the side and top edges and press the braid in place. Turn the braid under the bottom edge and staple or tack it in place. Staple or tack a tape to the bottom edge of the frame, to protect the fabrics from wear. Reassemble the panels to make the screen.

Edge-bound Towels

Choose contrasting or patterned fabrics, such as gingham or ticking as shown, to make a decorative edging for luxurious towels.

YOU WILL NEED

MATERIALS
towel
contrasting fabric
contrasting thread

EQUIPMENT
tape measure
scissors
pins
sewing machine
iron
needle

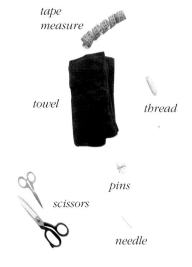

tape measure

towel

thread

pins

scissors

needle

fabric

1 Measure the towel and cut the contrasting fabric to this length, plus a 40 cm (16 in) extra allowance, by 6–8 cm (2¼–3¼ in) wide. Join the strips together on the shortest edge, with a 1 cm (½ in) seam allowance. To make a loop, cut another piece of contrasting fabric 20 cm (8 in) long and fold it in half lengthways. Machine stitch the long edge. Turn right sides out. Position, pin and tack (baste) the raw edges of the loop to the edge of the towel, in one corner or in the middle of one side.

CRAFT TIP
Gingham washes well so makes an ideal edging for towels.

2 Pin the edging with right sides facing, along the edge of the towel. At each corner, form an extra fold of fabric 1 cm (½ in) wide. Stitch along the seam line; make sure you don't stitch the folds.

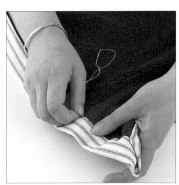

3 Press the edging out on the right side. Press the raw edges under 1 cm (½ in) accurately. Fold the edging over and pin it on the wrong side. Slip stitch the edging in place. In the corners, tuck the fold of fabric under, to form a diagonal seam. Ladder stitch or slip stitch the folded edges together.

Linen Bag

Choose ticking or another hard-wearing fabric and a fun trimming to make this bag. The lower half of the bag is lined.

YOU WILL NEED

MATERIALS
fabric
heavyweight interfacing
thread
trimming
cord

EQUIPMENT
tape measure
scissors
iron
sewing machine
pins
needle

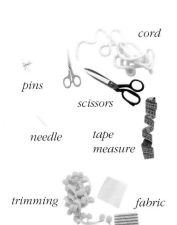

cord

pins

scissors

needle

tape measure

trimming

fabric

thread

1 To make the lined lower half of the bag, cut two fabric circles with a 30 cm (12 in) diameter. Cut two similar circles of interfacing. Cut two pieces of fabric, and two pieces of interfacing 99 x 24 cm (40 x 9½ in). Fuse the interfacing to the wrong side of the fabric pieces. Fold the rectangular pieces of fabric in half widthways, right sides together and machine stitch a seam along the short edge, to make a tube. Pin one edge of each tube around the raw edges of each circle piece, right sides together. Machine stitch the seams, clipping into the seam allowance.

CRAFT TIP
Remember to wash ticking before using (unless pre-shrunk) to check for shrinkage.

2 Cut a piece of fabric 99 x 45 cm (40 x 18 in). Fold in half lengthways, right sides together. Machine stitch the short edge. On the top edge, press a 6 mm (³⁄₁₆ in) wide hem to the wrong side, and then press another 3 cm (1¾ in) hem to the wrong side. Sew hems. With right sides together, machine stitch the top edge of the lower half of bag to the bottom edge of the tube.

3 Turn right sides out. Press to the wrong side of the top edge of the lining a turning of 2 cm (¾ in). Place the lining inside the bag and slip stitch the folded edge to the inside of the bag. Pin the trimming around seam line, and top edge of the tube. Machine stitch the trimming in place. Thread cord through casing and tie the ends.

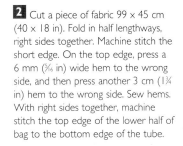

Covered Hat Box

Improve the appearance of a plain hat box,
to make an attractive accessory.

YOU WILL NEED

MATERIALS
cardboard hat box
fabric
double-sided sticky tape
glue
4 cm (1½ in) wide ribbon
self-adhesive felt
wadding (batting)

EQUIPMENT
craft knife or scalpel
tape measure
scissors
pinking shears

*tape
measure*

scissors

ribbon

glue

*double-sided
sticky tape*

fabric

*craft
knife*

*pinking
shears*

*self-adhesive
felt*

wadding

1 Cut two slits 4.5 cm wide by 1 cm deep (1¾ × ½ in) either side of the hat box. Measure the circumference and depth of the box. Cut one piece of fabric to twice the depth of the box plus 6 cm (2¼ in) by the circumference plus 3 cm (1¼ in).

2 Lay the fabric out right side down. Roll the box along it, sticking the fabric to the box with double-sided sticky tape. Clip into the seam allowance so that the fabric lies smoothly. Cut and tuck the fabric under at the top edge of the slit; glue and fix in place.

3 Spread a line of glue at the end of the ribbon, and fix it to the inside of the box, above the slit. Thread the ribbon through the slit. Tuck the fabric in at the lower edge of the slit and glue it in place. Repeat on the other side.

4 Fold the fabric over the rim of the box to the inside, clip into the seam allowance and stick the fabric to the bottom of the box with double-sided sticky tape. Cut out one piece of self-adhesive felt to the size of the base of the box, with pinking shears. Remove the paper backing and stick it to the inside of the box.

5 Cut one piece of wadding (batting) to the size of the lid. Spread some glue on the lid and stick the wadding (batting) to it. Cut one piece of fabric to the size of the lid plus 2 cm (¾ in) all round. Lay the fabric wrong side up, put the lid in position and fold the fabric over the edge. Stick it to the inside of the lid with double-sided sticky tape, clipping into the turning allowance.

6 Cut a piece of fabric to the length of the circumference of the lid plus a 4 cm (1½ in) overlap, by twice the depth of the rim of the lid. Fold fabric in half lengthways and press. Match fold to top edge of rim and stick right side of fabric to rim with tape. Fold raw edge over rim and stick it to the inside. Cut self-adhesive felt to size and stick to the inside of the lid.

Shelf Edging

Quick and simple, this scalloped edging makes a feature of an otherwise dull storage unit.

YOU WILL NEED

MATERIALS
graph paper
stencil paper or card (cardboard)
fabric
heavy-weight fusible interfacing
thread
bias binding

EQUIPMENT
tape measure
pencil
craft knife or scalpel
scissors
iron
sewing machine
fabric marker
pins

bias binding

interfacing

scissors

tape measure

needles

craft knife

graph paper

pins

fabric

fabric marker

1 Measure the shelf length. and count the scallops required. Divide width by this number and scale up template (pattern) on page 22 to this size. Cut template (pattern) from stencil paper. Cut a strip of fabric to shelf length, plus a 2 cm (¾ in) turning allowance, by 13 cm (5½ in), plus the depth of the shelf, plus a 2 cm (¾ in) hem allowance. Cut a strip of interfacing to the same size and iron to wrong side of fabric. On the top edge, press, pin and machine stitch a 1 cm (½ in) double hem.

2 Lay the fabric strip on the table. Mark around the template (pattern) with a fabric marker all along the length. Cut away the excess fabric.

3 Machine stitch the bias binding to the right side of the scalloped edge. Fold the bias binding over the fabric edge and slip stitch it to the wrong side.

4 Neaten the edging with a hem and pin it along the back edge of the shelf. Fold the fabric over the shelf edge and pin it at either side.

Fabric-covered Frame

Buy a ready-made wooden or plastic frame and remove the glass and backing. Choose a patterned or checked fabric to make this attractive ornament.

YOU WILL NEED

MATERIALS
wadding (batting)
ready-made wooden or
  plastic frame
fabric
fabric glue

EQUIPMENT
scissors
tape measure

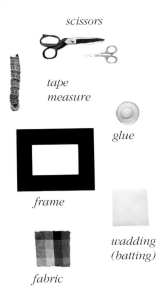

scissors

tape
measure

glue

frame

wadding
(batting)

fabric

1 Cut out one piece of wadding (batting) to the shape of the frame, and glue and press it to the top of the frame.

2 Cut one piece of fabric to the size of the frame, plus 4 cm (1½ in) all round. Lay the fabric wrong side up and place the frame face-down on it. Spread a line of glue down one side of the frame, on the back. Pull the fabric over the frame and press it in place. Repeat on the opposite edge.

3 Spread a line of glue on the top edge of the frame. Tuck in the corners of the fabric, pull the edge over and press it to the back of the frame.

4 Cut a slit in the centre of the fabric and snip into each inner corner of the frame, less 5 mm (¼ in). Spread a line of glue all around the inside edge of the frame, pull the fabric edges over and press them in place.

Fabric-covered Lampshade

Create an original lampshade by covering a frame with fabric that complements the room.

YOU WILL NEED

MATERIALS
conical lampshade frame
tape
thread
fabric
lining fabric
glue

EQUIPMENT
needles
tape measure
scissors
pins
fabric marker
sewing machine
iron
clothes pegs

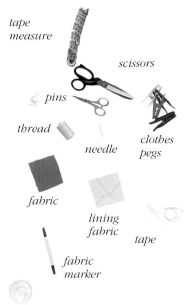

tape measure

scissors

pins

thread

needle

clothes pegs

fabric

lining fabric

tape

fabric marker

glue

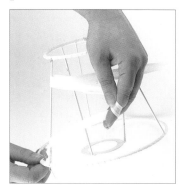

1 Wind the tape tightly around each strut and the ring of the frame. To finish the binding, tuck under the raw edges of the tapes and stitch them to the bound frame.

2 Measure the size of panel. Cut one piece of fabric on the cross (diagonal). Cut the fabric to the size of the panel, plus 3 cm (1¼ in) all round. Work around the frame, pinning the fabric over the top and bottom rings to the inside of the frame, pulling the fabric taut. Draw around the outline of the wire-framed panel with a fabric marker.

3 Unpin the fabric from the frame. Cut out the panel plus a 1.5 cm (⅝ in) seam allowance all round. Cut as many fabric panels as there are wire panels. With right sides together, pin and machine stitch the panels to form a tube. Turn to the right side and press.

4 Slip the fabric tube over the frame, aligning the seams with the upright struts. Oversew the fabric to the binding tape on the rings. Trim away the excess fabric from around the top and bottom rings, close to the stitching.

5 Place the lining fabric around the inside of the frame. Repeat steps 2 and 3. Make incisions in the lining so that it fits around the wire supports. Pin the lining fabric to the bound frame and oversew it all round. Trim the excess lining from the top and bottom rings.

6 Make bias binding from the main fabric (see page 20). Fold under the long edges and press them. Spread a line of glue on the bottom and top edges and fix the binding in place, overlapping the ends. Hold it in place with clothes pegs while it dries.

Pleated-paper Lampshade

Make a pleated lampshade from plain or patterned paper or cardboard. Choose a conical lampshade frame with bottom and top edges. Use lightbulbs of 60 watts or less.

YOU WILL NEED

MATERIALS
conical lampshade frame
paper or cardboard
glue
ribbon

EQUIPMENT
tape measure
craft knife or scalpel
pencil
metal rule
scissors
set square (carpenter's square)
hole punch

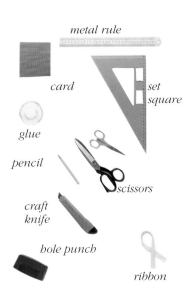

metal rule

card

set square

glue

pencil

scissors

craft knife

hole punch

ribbon

1 Measure the circumference of the lower edge of the frame. Multiply this measurement by two. Cut the paper or cardboard to this length, plus a 2 cm (¾ in) overlap, by the height. On the wrong wide, mark points 2 cm (¾ in) apart, with a pencil. To make pleats, match up the marks with a metal rule; draw a crease with the blunt end of scissors. Fold in the pleats.

2 To mark the position of the two rows of holes, make a template (pattern). Cut a piece of cardboard 2 x 5 cm (¾ x 2 in). With a hole punch, punch holes on the central line and 2 and 4 cm (¾ and 1½ in) from the top edge. Place the template (pattern) on the top edge of a folded pleat and mark the holes. With a hole punch, punch the pairs of holes in each pleat.

3 With a pair of scissors, cut across the lower row of holes to the inside of each pleat, except the end pleats.

4 To join the end pleats, spread a line of glue on to one side edge and press the other end in place. With a hole punch, punch the pair of holes.

5 Cut a piece of ribbon to the length of the shade and thread it through the upper row of holes. Draw up the ribbon, tie a knot and trim the ends.

6 Fit the lower row of holes over the upper ring of the lampshade frame. Spread the pleats out evenly.

PUBLISHER'S ACKNOWLEDGEMENTS

The Publisher would like to acknowledge the following companies for the use/loan of materials and accessories for projects featured in this book.

Weymess Houles (furnishing fabric suppliers)
40 Newman Street,
London,W1P 3PA.
Tel: 0171 255 3305

Ian Mankin (furnishing fabric suppliers)
109 Regents Park Road, London NW1 8UR. Tel: 0171 722 0997

McCulloch and Wallis (fabric and haberdashery suppliers)
25 Dering Street, London, W1.
Tel: 0171 629 0311

Dylon International Ltd (suppliers of dyes, fabric paints and pens) Worsley Bridge Road, London, SE26 5BE.
Tel: 0181 650 4801

D.M.C. Creative World Ltd (suppliers of embroidery threads)
62 Pullman Road,
Wigston,
Leicester, LE8 2DY.
Tel: 0116 2811040

Hallis Hudson Group Ltd (furnishing fabrics, trimming suppliers, curtain poles, tracks and accessories)
Bushell Street, Preston,
PR1 2SP.
Tel: 01772 202202

Emma Bernhardt (imported PVC fabrics suppliers)
Tel: 0171 935 6802

DNA (artificial trees)
13 Hollingbourne Avenue,
Herne Hill, London, SE24 9BN.
Tel: 0171 978 8739

Janine Ferris (Metal frames)
Tel: 0171 978 8739

C.I. Davis & Co Ltd (suppliers of silk fabrics)
94/96 Seymour Place,
London, W1H 5DG.
Tel: 0171 723 0895

Contributors: Angela Hauch (Knitted cushion) Tel: 0181 541 0538

Stylists: Theressa Allflatt, Kirsty Turner, and Lindy Leyton

Author Acknowledgements
My thanks and gratitude to Helen Sudell at Anness Publishing, James Duncan for his continual optimism, Theressa Allflatt for support and enthusiasm. Also Clare Fletcher, Clare Buckle, Tim Ward and Carol Rubra.